# At the

# Table of the Lord

## by Dr. Richard D. Dobbins

*Foreword by Rev. Robert D. Crabtree*
*Superintendent, Ohio District Council of the Assemblies of God*

*"Reflections" by Rev. J. Donald McManness*
*Executive Secretary, Ohio District Council of the Assemblies of God*

Totally Alive Publications
Akron, Ohio

ISBN # 1-890329-67-3

# Table of Contents

# Dedication

This book is dedicated to the following servants of our Lord:

- Rev. Robert D. Crabtree, Superintendent of the Ohio District Council of the Assemblies of God, at whose suggestion it was published.

- The Ohio District Presbytery Board, who agreed to fund its publication.

- The ministers and spouses of the Ohio District who gave me the honor of serving as their Assistant District Superintendent for 30 years.

- Priscilla, my wife, whose patience and inspiration encouraged me in completing this project.

# Foreword

Imagine yourself sitting with hundreds of ministers and their spouses at an annual state conference. Eyes are fixed on the speaker, Dr. Richard D. Dobbins, as he preaches his annual Communion message. In a variety of unique ways, he has just described the crucifixion of our Lord and Savior, Jesus Christ. Some ministers are sitting in deep contemplation; others are busily taking notes so they can share the richness of Dr. Dobbins' ministry with their own congregations.

For 30 years, Dr. Richard Dobbins has served as the Assistant Superintendent of the Ohio District Council of the Assemblies of God—and for 30 years his Communion messages have been a highlight of our Ohio District Council meetings. This book includes some of those Communion messages.

The life and ministry of Dr. Dobbins has greatly impacted not only the Ohio District Council, but the entire General Council of the Assemblies of God. As founder and president of EMERGE Ministries Mental Health Resource Center in Akron, Ohio, for the past 25 years he and his staff have provided a variety of counseling services to more than 1,500 ministers and thousands of other believers.

Dr. Dobbins has authored many books and produced a number of video and audio tape series on subjects of direct benefit to ministers and the congregations they serve. This book adds to that outstanding collection of resources. EMERGE Ministries also provides ministers and counselors with an opportunity for advanced training in pastoral counseling.

He has practiced what he preaches. He showed us how to hold steady in one's faith and let go of a beloved spouse when it became obvious that his first wife, Dolores, was about to be ushered into the presence of the Lord. And then we watched with joy as God blessed him with a wonderful new love and ministry partner, the former Priscilla Adams. Priscilla became Mrs. Richard Dobbins on April 2, 1994. Together, they continue to minister the good mental health news of the gospel.

Dr. Dobbins is a frequent guest on various television and radio programs. Currently, he is the radio voice of the Assemblies of God, heard across the nation with Pastor Jerry Qualls, the co-host of *From This Day Forward*.

On behalf of the Ohio District Council and especially the members of the Ohio District Presbytery Board, I want to thank Dr. Dobbins for 30 years of unselfish service and faithful support as our Assistant District Superintendent. He has been a terrific advisor and counselor to me in my duties as Ohio District Superintendent. And more than that, he has become one of my best friends.

*Rev. Robert D. Crabtree*
*Superintendent, Ohio District Council*
*of the Assemblies of God*

# Reflections on the Ministry of
# Dr. Richard D. Dobbins

Dr. Richard D. Dobbins was granted a license to preach by the Illinois District Council of the Assemblies of God in 1946 and was ordained in that district in May of 1949. His early ministry was in evangelism. It was my privilege to hear Dr. Dobbins at a fellowship meeting in Granite City, Illinois, in 1948. This was during the time of the so-called "Latter Rain" movement. To this day, I remember the subject of Dr. Dobbins' message. He preached about the danger of putting new wine into old wineskins and sewing a new patch on an old garment—a timely message. Even at that early age, Dr. Dobbins was an impressive and powerful speaker.

Dr. Dobbins transferred to the Ohio District in January, 1951, after starting a church in South Akron. A cooperative church for three years, this church became affiliated with the Ohio District Council of the Assemblies of God in June, 1953.

In 1958, South Akron Assembly of God, as it was called then, merged with Central Assembly of God, resulting in The Assembly of God at Brown and Vine (a new name which reflected the street names at the corner where it was located). In 1965, the name of the church was changed to Evangel Temple Assembly of God when a new building was erected at 688 Dan Street. This location is still the home of Evangel Temple.

Early in his pastoral ministry, Dr. Dobbins developed an interest in merging the concepts of psychology with a Christian perspective and began to study at The University of Akron. He received his doctorate from The University of Akron in 1970. During the time of his pastoral ministry at Evangel Temple, he developed an extensive counseling ministry among parishioners of the church and with other people who sought his help. In 1976, Dr. Dobbins resigned his pastorate and became the full-time director of EMERGE Ministries, a Christian counseling ministry that continues to the present day.

Dr. Dobbins was elected as the Assistant Superintendent of the Ohio District Council in 1969 and has served for 30 years in that position.

In addition, he has served on numerous committees and has developed many programs and manuals for use in the District office and in our churches. He has served as the chairman of the Ohio District Finance Committee from 1966 until the present. He also served on the Board of Regents for Northeast Bible Institute and on many General Council committees. Bro. Dobbins has enjoyed a unique relationship with the Foreign Missions Department of the General Council of the Assemblies of God and has counseled many missionaries over the years.

It would be impossible to fully describe the ministry and contribution of Dr. Dobbins to the ministers and lay people of the Ohio District. One of the high points of his ministry has been the Communion service for Ohio District Council, where he has spoken for the last 30 years. This service, which deeply touches the lives of the participants, is a spiritually moving experience which is always made fresh by an anointed message from God's Word.

His ministry at EMERGE is so well known that he is in great demand around the world. Eternity alone will reveal the extent of the influence he has had on the lives of the people with whom he has come in contact.

On the whimsical side, it was interesting to note that, in 1957, Bro. Dobbins' credentials were sent to the District and forwarded on to the General Council offices in Springfield, Missouri for renewal. However, the certificate was lost in the mail and it was necessary to issue a replacement certificate.

Likewise, in 1960 a letter from the District secretary to Bro. Dobbins indicated that his renewal application had not been received and stated, "I began to wonder if it were possible that your renewal application could have been in the mail which was stolen from our box on September 10." A hurried renewal was returned promptly and credentials issued before the deadline.

Another interesting item in the files is that in the years 1951-1954, Bro. Dobbins was supported by freewill offerings or a portion of the tithes, but he was finally salaried by his church in 1955. That must have been quite an accomplishment.

Along with a host of others who have known him in a personal way over the years, I have the deepest respect for this man of God, who set his goal on a unique and vital ministry early in life. He persevered to develop that ministry, even during a time when it was not popular to do so, and has over the years shown the effectiveness of what God can do through a man dedicated to Him.

*Rev. J. Donald McManness*
*Executive Secretary of the Ohio District Council*
*of the Assemblies of God*

# Introduction

Even though leading the Communion service at our annual District Council has been an awesome responsibility, I have always looked forward to it. During my 26 years in pastoral ministry, I placed great importance on the healing potential of the Communion service. Now, as a Christian psychologist, I am even more convinced that much of the therapy that takes place in our offices would be unnecessary if the Church were more alert to the healing potential present in the Communion service.

The pastor who encourages people to be vulnerable to God and transparent about their sins will be rewarded by seeing many of them relieved of guilt, anger, fear, and depression during their observance of Communion. He will also discover that the reconciliation of badly stressed or broken marriage and family relationships often begins in decisions made during a Communion service.

Ministers and church leaders benefit greatly from the healing impact of a Communion service such as this one, conducted especially for them. That is why this responsibility has been so awesome for me. Throughout the year, I would seek the Lord's guidance in determining the direction this service should take. At times, I would get the inspiration for the Communion message early in the year. Other times, I would be putting the finishing touches on my notes the evening before the service.

With the exception of one or two, these sermons were prepared exclusively for this annual occasion. This was the only time they were preached, because the messages God gave me were especially for this group.

When our Ohio District Superintendent, Rev. Robert Crabtree, suggested that the Ohio District Presbytery Board authorize funds for the publication of these messages, I was surprised. I want to take this opportunity to thank the District leadership and the Presbytery Board for providing the funds for the publication of this book. It is a joy to share these messages with you.

I have engaged in only minor editing, in order to retain as much of the original spirit of the services as possible. Some of the taped service transcripts included times of prayer and the actual serving of Communion; some included our congregational singing during Communion; others did not. They are presented in this book in their entirety as they were recorded over the years, with only a few explanatory notes added.

My prayer is that the content of these messages will continue to promote health and healing throughout the Body of Christ as they are read and now shared from other pulpits.

*Dr. Richard D. Dobbins*

# 1

# Finding Your Place at the Table of the Lord *

Observing Communion is always special to me, whether I am a guest speaker for someone else, in my own home church with my pastor, or at a couples retreat where my wife and I enjoy the Lord's Supper alone together. Another very special observance of Communion is this time of year when we meet at the Lord's Table as brothers and sisters in the ministry, along with delegates from our various local churches.

This morning, we're going to look at John's account of the very first observance of the Lord's Supper:

> *"Now before the feast of the Passover, when Jesus knew that His hour was come that He should depart out of this world unto the Father, having loved His own which were in the world, He loved them unto the end. And supper being ended, the devil having now put into the heart of Judas Iscariot, Simon's son, to betray him;*

> *"Jesus knowing that the Father had given all things into His hands, and that He was come from God, and went to God; He riseth from supper, and laid aside His garments; and took a towel, and girded himself. After that he poureth water into a basin, and began to wash the disciples' feet, and to wipe them with the towel wherewith He was girded . . .*

---

\* Sermon for the Communion Service of the 1985 Ohio District Council of the Assemblies of God, Christian Life Center, Dayton, Ohio.

*"So after He had washed their feet, and had taken His garments, and was set down again, he said unto them . . .*

*"Verily, verily, I say unto you, that one of you shall betray me. Then the disciples looked one on another, doubting of whom He spake. Now there was leaning on Jesus' bosom one of His disciples, whom Jesus loved. Simon Peter therefore beckoned to him, that he should ask who it should be of whom he spake. He then lying on Jesus' breast saith unto Him, Lord, who is it? Jesus answered, He it is, to whom I shall give a sop, when I have dipped it. And when He had dipped the sop, He gave it to Judas Iscariot, the son of Simon. And after the sop Satan entered into him. Then said Jesus unto him, That thou doest, do quickly.*

*"Now no man at the table knew for what intent He spake this unto him. For some of them thought, because Judas had the bag, that Jesus had said unto him, Buy those things that we have need of against the feast; or, that he should give something to the poor. He then having received the sop went immediately out: and it was night."*[1]

As you might expect, John gives us the most intimate, personal view of the Last Supper found among the gospels. He shows us how close Jesus was to each of His disciples. From Jesus' perspective, there was no "distance" between Him and them. Even though He knew one of them would deny Him and another would betray Him, He humbled himself to wash the feet of each disciple.

### Jesus did not leave anyone out

(In Leonardo da Vinci's 1498 painting of The Last Supper, which is undoubtedly the most famous of many artists' conceptions of this event, Judas is seated between John and Peter. John sits next to Jesus. The moment in time that da Vinci chose to portray in his painting is the disciples' reaction to Jesus' announcement that one of them would betray Him. While the other 11 apostles' faces are clearly visible, registering shock and disbelief, Judas appears to be trying to avoid the light, speaking to no one. Although the pouch of money—30 pieces of silver—is clearly visible in his right hand, he is not singled out as the betrayer.)[3]

When Jesus announced that one them would betray Him, Simon Peter prompted John to ask, *"Lord, who is it?"* The sensitivity Jesus showed even to Judas' feelings in responding to John's question is still touching today. He responded in a way that seemed to protect Judas. At the time, not one of the disciples was aware of the reason Judas left the table, except perhaps John.[2]

Not one of Jesus' disciples was left out of the first Communion service. Peter would deny Him and Judas would betray Him, but Jesus washed the feet of both of them.

If you read the gospel accounts of the Last Supper, and then read Paul's account of it in 1 Corinthians 11, you will find that each writer offers a slightly different description of the conversation and events that evening. Matthew and John gave eyewitness accounts; Mark, Luke, and Paul shared what they learned by divine inspiration.

Matthew gives more detail of Judas' plans immediately prior to the Passover meal and even mentions the price paid him for his betrayal of Jesus: 30 pieces of silver. Luke calls attention to the disciples' *"strife"* as they argued over which of them should be accounted the greatest of the group. All of the gospels tell of Peter's emphatic promise never to deny or abandon Jesus and the Master's response. Some mention the foot-washing that evening, and others don't.

John (among others) draws attention to the seating arrangement at the table. Of necessity, the disciples were physically seated at various distances from the Master. Not all of them could be physically by His side at the same time. But John also addressed a far more important kind of *distance* at the table.

### Spiritual distance between the disciples and Jesus

John shares with us the *spiritual* distance between the disciples and Jesus, revealed by the inquiries five of these men made after Jesus announced that one of them would betray Him. John asked Him, *"Lord, who is it?"*[4] Peter asked, *"Whither goest thou?"* and *"Why cannot I follow Thee now?"*[5] Thomas asked, *"Lord, we know not whither thou goest; and how can we know the way?"*[6] Philip pleads, *"Shew us the Father, and it sufficeth us."*[7] And Judas (not Judas Iscariot) said, *"Lord, how is it that thou wilt manifest thyself unto us, and not unto the world?"*[8]

For three years, these men had been with the Lord. They had heard
Him teach. They had seen His miracles. They were the ones to whom
Jesus would entrust the future of His kingdom. Thus their spiritual
ignorance, given their proximity and exposure to Jesus' life and ministry,
was truly amazing.

In the Lord's reaction to these remarks, He tells His disciples how
important it is for them to narrow the distance between Him and them.
He offers a new commandment as a remedy to their situation. *"A new
commandment I give unto you, that ye love one another; as I have loved
you, that ye also love one another. By this shall all men know that ye are
my disciples, if ye have love one to another."*[9]

Although Jesus was equally available for a spiritually intimate
relationship with each of His disciples, they were at varying spiritual
distances from Him. John, the disciple *"whom Jesus loved,"* who was
on the very closest terms with the Lord, was willing to speak aloud the
question that was on Peter's mind: *"Lord, who is it?"*[10] Perhaps John
already knew the identity of the betrayer; perhaps he didn't.

At the other end of the spiritual spectrum, Judas—portrayed by da
Vinci as sitting next to John—already held the payment for betrayal in
his hand. *He even brought it with him to the Passover—that's how far he
had spiritually distanced himself from the Lord.* In between were all the
other disciples with their concerns over who was most valuable to the
kingdom of God; who would have preeminence among them; and finally
their concern over any spiritual responsibility they might bear for the
betrayal.

### Spiritual competition in the institutional church

The institutional church, unfortunately, still endures spiritual
competition among brothers and sisters in ministry as to who will have
the pre-eminence or *be the greatest* among us. But those who look beyond
the institutional church to the message of Scripture can see that the
position John occupied at the Last Supper is available to each of us.
There is room on Jesus' breast for each of us. Each of us can hear His
heartbeat if we are willing to risk getting that close. Each of us can
become intimately aware of His Spirit and His love.

### The secret of unity in the church

The secret of unity among us is not to focus on our relative positions in the institutional church; rather, we need to focus on the spiritual distance between ourselves and the Lord. There is little any of us can do to convince another his theology is wrong or that any one of us is more valuable to the Lord than another.

However, each of us can close the distance between our own self and the Lord. Each of us can find our place on His bosom and near His heart. When we do this, He brings us closer to each other and gives us the unity of heart and purpose we need to do His work. Our love for each other demonstrated in this way will give the world visible evidence of our love for Him—and His for them.

At Christ's right hand, Leonardo da Vinci placed John next to the Master, followed by Judas, Peter, Andrew, James the Greater, and Bartholomew (at Christ's far right). On His left side, da Vinci portrayed James the Less, Thomas, Philip, Matthew, Jude, and Simon (at Christ's far left.) I don't know how he decided where to place the various apostles around the Lord's Table in his painting.[11] I do know, however, that each of us has both the opportunity and the responsibility for finding our own place at the Lord's Table today. Each of us knows what must be removed from our own heart in order to be as close as we possibly can be to Jesus.

And so, as Paul admonishes us," *Let a man examine himself, and so let him eat of that bread, and drink of that cup.* "[12] This morning, may each of us remove anything that is between us and our Lord. May we let this moment of intimate love between His heart and ours remind us that our relationship is not simply an institutional one. It goes far beyond having our name on the membership list of any church or religious governing body.

We are members of His body, of His flesh, and of His bones.[13] Because of the closeness of our relationship with Him, we have a place all our own to find . . . at the Lord's Table.

---

[1] John 13:1-5,12,21-30.
[2] John 13:23-29.

[3] Heydenreich, Ludwig H. **Leonardo: The Last Supper**. New York: Viking Press, 1974.

[4] John 13:25.

[5] John 13:36, 37.

[6] John 14:5.

[7] John 14:8.

[8] John 14:22.

[9] John 13:34, 35.

[10] John 13:23-25.

[11] Leonardo da Vinci's **The Last Supper** was painted near the close of the 15th century on a wall of the Refectory (dining hall) of Santa Maria della Grazie monastery, near Milan, Italy. Students of da Vinci's life and work generally credit him with being a serious student of the gospels and very knowledgeable about Scripture. Apparently the seating choice was his own rather than that of whoever commissioned this painting. Leonardo da Vinci is believed to be the first artist to paint the moment of Christ's announcement about one of the disciples planning to betray Him.

Heydenreich, who has made a lifetime study of Leonardo da Vinci's work in general and this painting in particular, calls the moment expressed in this painting (p. 67,68) a " . . . momentary pause between two great emotions"—those being tranquility and the horror that had startled the apostles out of their tranquility into a wide cross-current of different emotions which were just beginning to surface on their faces. The impact of this announcement was surely of the same magnitude as one that had come before it (when angels announced the impending birth of Jesus) and one that would come after it (when angels would announce to the women at the garden tomb, "He is not here, for He is risen as He said").

[12] I Corinthians 11:28.

[13] Ephesians 5:30.

# 2

# At the Table of the Lord *

*"Now the first day of the feast of unleavened bread the disciples came to Jesus, saying unto Him, Where wilt thou that we prepare for thee to eat the passover? And He said, Go into the city to such a man, and say unto him, The Master saith, my time is at hand; I will keep the passover at thy house with my disciples. And the disciples did as Jesus had appointed them; and they made ready the passover.*

*"Now when the even was come, he sat down with the twelve. And as they did eat, he said, Verily I say unto you, that one of you shall betray me. And they were exceeding sorrowful, and began every one of them to say unto him, Lord, is it I? And He answered and said, He that dippeth his hand with me in the dish, the same shall betray me. The Son of man goeth as it is written of him: but woe unto that man by whom the Son of man is betrayed! it had been good for that man if he had not been born. Then Judas, which betrayed him, answered and said, Master is it I? He said unto him, Thou hast said.*

*"And as they were eating, Jesus took bread, and blessed it, and brake it, and gave it to the disciples, and said, Take, eat; this is my body. And he took the cup, and gave thanks, and gave it to them, saying, Drink ye all of it; For this is my blood of the new testament which is shed for many for the remission of sins. But I say unto you, I will not drink henceforth of this fruit of the vine, until that day when I drink it new with you in my Father's*

---

* Sermon for the Communion Service of the 1986 Ohio District Council of the Assemblies of God, Calvary Assembly of God, Youngstown, Ohio.

*kingdom. And when they had sung an hymn, they went out into the Mount of Olives."* [1]

Within 1500 years after that very simple beginning of our Lord's celebration of Passover with His disciples, the Lord's Table became a controversial and divisive subject in the institutional church. The Roman Catholic Church took the position that with each celebration of the Eucharist or Lord's Supper, the body of Christ was broken again and the blood of Christ was spilled again. They believe that during the act of blessing the elements at each celebration of the Eucharist, the bread literally becomes the body of Christ and the wine literally becomes the blood of Christ. Theologians refer to this Catholic position as *transubstantiation.*

Our Reformation brethren took issue with several areas of the Catholic faith—this one among them. Some of the reformers argued that the Communion bread does not become the literal body of Christ, but the body of Christ is present *with* the bread. And the Communion cup does not become the literal blood of the Lord, but the blood of the Lord is present *with* the cup. Theologians refer to this doctrine as *consubstantiation.*

Some of the more radical brethren were determined to put even more distance between them and the Catholic church. They said the bread is not the physical body of Christ and the body of Christ is also not present with the bread; the cup is not the blood of the Lord and the blood of the Lord is not present with the cup. These reformers saw the bread and the cup simply as emblems—*symbols meant to remind participants of the Last Supper and its significance for believers throughout their earthly life.*

This debate over the elements of Communion continues today. There is further dispute among us as to whether we should eat from one loaf or each have a separate wafer; whether we should drink from the same cup or each have a separate cup; whether we should serve communion once a week, once a month, or twice a year.

### The central purpose of Communion

All of these theological controversies tend to detract from the central purpose of Communion: "let a man examine himself." [2] *This* is the sobering challenge of Communion! It is all too easy for us to let the elements of Communion become so common that we no longer discern *any* representation or reminder of the Lord's body in the bread . . . of the Lord's blood in the cup. When we no longer discern these elements to be other than simply the bread and the cup, how does it benefit us to participate in this commandment of our Lord?

So, this morning, I am calling each of us to self-examination. Just as we wash our hands before we sit down to partake of an earthly table, so we need to examine ourselves and experience cleansing of the heart before we approach the Lord's Table.

### A look at the past

Reflect for a few moments on your life. Look at the part of it that is behind you. In the work God has called me to do, it is my responsibility to sit with many of God's people who carry with them still-gaping wounds from the past. Many of these people are in the ministry. Many of the wounds they carry are rooted in things for which God forgave them long ago—but for which they have never been able to forgive themselves.

These people who insist on keeping old wounds open don't realize they are acting as if their conscience were more holy than God's character. The blood of Christ satisfied the holy character of God on their behalf, and He forgave them, but they still have a very sick need to punish themselves. This unresolved guilt from the past becomes a great weight that the enemy uses to drag them down and defeat them in the race God has set before them.

So, this morning, I ask that we look at our past. Let us be sure that every part of our past has been brought under the blood of Jesus Christ, God's Son. Let each of us be sure that our heart's door is wide open to Him who stands and so gently knocks. Let us be sure that there are no bars of gold or shekels of silver hidden in the floor of our tent. Let us allow the Lord who loved us enough to die for us to enter into every room of our past. Remember—He will never force himself into any area of your life or mine. He waits for an invitation.

While we pray for the blood of Christ to cleanse our past, let us also celebrate the many times when His body has been the source of healing for us and for members of our family. Let us think of those moments when His healing presence relieved us of our burdens and anxieties.

Last night when I got word that my grandson had been rushed to the hospital, I was reminded of how quickly this kind of unexpected news can change our world. The "important" issues of life are almost instantly reorganized and rearranged. Let us not take for granted the many times Christ's broken body has availed to touch our loved ones, to meet us in moments of great anxiety, and to provide a healing touch in our own body. We are here this morning celebrating the life and strength that comes to us from His body.

### A look at the present

Each of us also needs to focus on the present, as well as the past. It would be naïve of me to believe I am speaking to people who have no hidden secrets—whose lives consist *only* of that which pleases the Lord. For, at EMERGE we counsel hundreds of ministers a year. If their lives were filled only with thoughts and actions pleasing to the Lord, very few of them would ever need our help. In this regard, we in the ministry are no different from lay people who neglect the opportunity to cleanse their hearts at the table of the Lord. Our spiritual condition, our marriage, and our family relationships are just as much at risk as those of lay people when we and our spouses fail to make a daily application of the emblems of the Lord's broken body and shed blood to our lives.

I am sure there are those among us this morning who desperately need to discern Christ's body in this wafer; Christ's blood in this cup; who need to resolve issues between them and the Lord before an embarrassing cock-crowing brings them to the attention of the public. Paul reminds us that if we judge ourselves, others won't have to do it for us.[3] So, let us bring those difficult spiritual and emotional issues of our lives to Christ for cleansing by His blood. If you are weak in body this morning, may the Bread become life, strength, and healing to you.

### A look at the future

Also, as we celebrate at the Lord's Table today, may we anticipate the future He has planned for us in Christ. Seldom, when we take the bread and the cup, do we stop to remember that this celebrations links us with a family of brothers and sisters in Christ that has been growing for almost 2,000 years. More of this family is in heaven than is on earth at this moment. These are our brothers and sisters for whom time is no more; they are now with that great *"cloud of witnesses"* Paul wrote about.[4] There is no past, present, or future for them. They know now *even as they are known.* If they were able to communicate to us what they know, it would greatly relieve our anxiety. From their perspective, they could help us reorder our priorities so much more wisely . . . help us not to burden ourselves with so many things of a trivial and passing nature.

If Jesus tarries in His return to earth, we will be *privileged* to join this group some day. None of us know when we may be called to join them. Unless we live until the time of Jesus' Second Coming, each of us each has an "appointment in Samarra"[5] at some moment in time.

While I try to live as though my Lord will return for me at any second, I also realize that I may die of natural causes or accidental means before I take my next breath. When and if I leave this world by death, I do not want to feel the Lord has failed me either because He did not heal me or because He did not return to earth during my lifetime. I do not want to look at death as a defeat or disappointment. After all, death should be the ultimate victory for the child of God. It carries us into the presence of the Lord and puts us beyond the reach of temptation and sin. I would rather be *reconciled to the thought of dying* and be *surprised by the Second Coming of the Lord* than to be so convinced the Lord will return during my lifetime that I am surprised by and unprepared for my death.

Examine your life. Each of us needs to examine our ambitions, our goals, our dreams; to ask ourselves honestly whether, if we were offered a choice between having our ultimate earthly dreams fulfilled and being ushered into the presence of the Lord, we could say sincerely that *"to depart, and to be with Christ . . . is far better."*[6] Could you— could I—honestly say, *"For me to live is Christ, and to die is gain"?*[7]

As we come to His Table this morning, let us remember that first group of believers who sat at the Passover table with Him. Jesus told them that one of them would betray Him. Looking at each other in disbelief, they asked themselves and Him that soul-searching question,

*"Lord, is it I?"*[8] We need to examine ourselves. We need to bring any hint of betrayal by our past behavior under the sanctifying power of the blood of Jesus. We need to experience His forgiveness and be released from unnecessary burdens the enemy would thrust upon us.

We must also bring our present life to him today in an attitude of honest confession. He wants to forgive our sins—and He doesn't want to make it difficult for us. All we have to do is sincerely ask. Just like everyone else, we must remember that, *"If we say we have no sin, we deceive ourselves, and the truth is not in us."* However, the continuation of that passage reminds us that, *"If we confess our sins, he is faithful and just to forgive us our sins, and cleanse us from all unrighteousness."*[9]

And may the Lord make us extremely aware that we are a living link in an eternal chain of believers who will not cease praying and working until Jesus reigns completely over our lives and over our planet; until, *". . . the kingdoms of this world are become the kingdoms of our Lord, and of his Christ. . . ."*[10]

Each of us needs to *"so examine"* our own past, our present, and our future as we prepare to approach the Lord's Table together. Shall we bow our hearts in prayer.

*Oh, God, You loved us enough to send Your only begotten Son even though You knew He would be betrayed by us, denied by us, and nailed to a cruel cross for us. We don't understand love like that. And You did all of that, Lord, while we were still sinners who were reviling Your Name, desecrating Your gift of life, and abusing Your temple of the Holy Spirit. Oh, God, help us remember how we brought our shameful, sinful past to You when we were still your unredeemed enemies and found You loving enough to forgive us. Reassure us that surely now, as Your children, we can still safely bring our sins to You. Help us rise up against the enemy who would make us hide behind the trees of our own pride, trying to cover our sins and being preoccupied with our failures.*

*Lord, we rebuke the enemy this morning. We triumph over him as we bring the Lord of Calvary into every room of our lives, into every shadow of our hearts. Oh, may the blood of Jesus cleanse us today from all our sins. May we hold nothing from you today, God, but may we lay it all—in this moment of transparent honesty and repentance—before you today.*

*Visit us personally and intimately in this moment this morning, so that none, Lord, will leave with the burden of his sin, and none will leave in the darkness of his own heart. May we all walk in the light as You are in the Light and may we may have true fellowship with You and with one another as the blood of Jesus Christ, God's Son, cleanses us from all sins.*

*Father, we think of those among us who are spiritually and emotionally afflicted as we celebrate Your broken body and thank You for the gift of health and strength. May gifts of healing come from Your body, divided to each of us severally as the Holy Spirit would direct. Touch us and quicken us today.*

*May this cup be more to us than juice. May this wafer may be more to us than ordinary bread. May we discern in these emblems the body of our Lord which was broken for us and the blood of Jesus which was shed for us. May we examine ourselves so that nothing in our lives will stand in the way of Your mercy coming to us. May we examine ourselves so that Your life and all of its fullness may come to us. When we have partaken of the bread and the cup, may we lift our hearts and let the gates of our souls swing open as the King of Glory comes to fully possess these temples of the Holy Spirit. Make us vessels through which the life and love of Jesus can flow to a dark world. These things we pray in Jesus' name and for His glory. Amen.*

### Communion

*" . . . The Lord Jesus the same night in which he was betrayed took bread: And when he had given thanks, he brake it, and said, Take, eat: this is my body, which is broken for you: this do in remembrance of me."*[11]

Shall we eat together.

And now, let's have special prayer over the cup before we partake of it this morning:

*Lord, what we hold in our hand is not just juice, not just any cup, but it is an emblem of something far more precious and powerful,*

*designed to quicken our memories of the cleansing, forgiving grace of
God that comes to us through the blood of Jesus. And as we drink of this
cup this morning, let prison doors be shut behind us, let shackles fall
off, let chains be broken. Cleanse us anew and afresh. Give us victory,
Lord, that we can  take from this place and share with others as we
celebrate Your kingdom anew in our hearts. We confess our sins, and we
find You right now to be faithful and just to forgive us our sins and to
cleanse us from all unrighteousness as You bless this cup to our lives. In
Jesus' Name, Amen.*

*"And he took the cup, and gave thanks, and gave it to them,
saying, Drink ye all of it; For this is my blood of the new testament,
which is shed for many for the remission of sins."*[12]

Shall we drink together.

As you have opened your hearts to the Lord, He has come and
cleansed you. He has come and touched you. Therefore, let your heart
respond with praise and rejoice in His Name. For as you are a partaker
of His grace, this fresh touch of His grace upon your life will generate
within others a response that will help them open their lives. This is how
the River of Life flows. The blood of Christ cleanses both shepherd and
sheep. As His grace is real to our hearts, we will be able to make His
grace real to others. He has heard your prayer this morning. He has
responded to the cry of your heart and He has cast aside your burden. He
has relieved you of the shackles and He has opened your prison door. He
has shut the gate of your past, made straight the way of your present, and
opened wide the door to the future He has planned for you.

Rejoice in the victory He has given you over the enemy. For, no
enemy can take from you what God has given you. Greater is He that is
in you than he that is in the world. You can overcome that lion that seeks
to devour you. You can overcome the thief that seeks to steal from you.
You can overcome him by the blood of the Lamb and by the word of
your testimony. So shall the Lord seal His victory in your heart today.

---

[1] Matthew 26:17-30.
[2] 1 Corinthians 11:28.

[3] 1 Corinthians 11:28-31.

[4] Hebrews 12:1.

[5] From a scene in English writer W. Somerset Maugham's play, "Sheppey," where Death makes herself known to a rich man's servant in the marketplace one morning with a beckoning gesture. The servant, surprised and frightened, borrows his master's horse to ride to far away Samarra in the hope that Death cannot find him there. Later that same day, Death encounters the servant's master and says, by way of explanation, that the gesture merely expressed her surprise at finding the servant still in Baghdad that morning, ". . . for I have an appointment with him tonight in Samarra."

[6] Philippians 1:23.

[7] Philippians 1:21.

[8] Matthew 26:22.

[9] 1 John 1:7-9.

[10] Revelation 11:15.

[11] 1 Corinthians 11:23,24.

[12] Matthew 26:27,28.

# 3

# Chastened . . . but Not Condemned *

"Know ye not that they which run in a race run all, but one receiveth the prize? So run, that ye may obtain.

"And every man that striveth for the mastery is temperate in all things. Now they do it to obtain a corruptible crown; but we an incorruptible. I therefore so run, not as uncertainly; so fight I, not as one that beateth the air: But I keep under my body, and bring it into subjection: lest that by any means, when I have preached to others, I myself should be a castaway.

"Moreover, brethren, I would not that ye should be ignorant, how that all our fathers were under the cloud, and all passed through the sea; And were all baptized unto Moses in the cloud and in the sea; And did all eat the same spiritual meat; And did all drink the same spiritual drink: for they drank of that spiritual Rock that followed them: and that Rock was Christ. But with many of them God was not well pleased: for they were overthrown in the wilderness.

"Now these things were our examples, to the intent we should not lust after evil things, as they also lusted. Neither be ye idolaters, as were some of them; as it is written, The people sat down to eat and drink, and rose up to play. Neither let us commit fornication, as some of them committed, and fell in one day three and twenty thousand. Neither let us tempt Christ, as

* Sermon for the Communion Service of the 1987 Ohio District Council of the Assemblies of God, Tri County Assembly of God, Fairfield, Ohio.

*some of them also tempted, and were destroyed of serpents.
Neither murmur ye, as some of them also murmured, and were
destroyed of the destroyer.*

*"Now all these things happened unto them for
ensamples: and they are written for our admonition, upon whom
the ends of the world are come. Wherefore let him that thinketh
he standeth take heed lest he fall. There hath no temptation taken
you but such as is common to man: but God is faithful, who will
not suffer you to be tempted above that ye are able; but will with
the temptation also make a way to escape, that ye may be able
to bear it. Wherefore, my dearly beloved, flee from idolatry. I
speak as to wise men; judge ye what I say.*

*"The cup of blessing which we bless, is it not the
communion of the blood of Christ? The bread which we break,
is it not the communion of the body of Christ? For we being
many are one bread, and one body: for we are all partakers of
that one bread."*[1]

In looking to the Lord for what He would have me share with
you today, I thought of how Paul addresses the subject of Communion in
1 Corinthians, chapters 9 and 10. In this letter, Paul is addressing the
need for healing the divisions among the Corinthian church.[2] Chapters
9-13 emphasize the need for unifying the body of Christ. This is a message
we sorely need at this moment in time.

A few weeks ago I purchased newsstand copies of U.S. News
and World Report, Time, and Newsweek—all of them featuring
Assemblies of God ministers. I also saw the same kind of embarrassing
display on the front of The National Enquirer and The Star at the
supermarket checkout stand. And I said to myself, *There simply has to
be a better way to conduct oneself and one's ministry!*

At the time, I was doing a personal study on how the Early Church
managed problems of personal discipline, and was reminded that our
walk with God is a very private, personal affair. Periodically, we who
are in full-time ministry must allow the Holy Spirit to lead us into serious
self-examination. During these times, we need to remind ourselves that
*our walk with God* is more important to Him—and to our own spiritual
health—than our work for Him.

It is so easy for us to judge each other by the results of our work. We strive for visible results. Please don't misunderstand me—the Lord, too, is desirous of fruit. But before He looks for the fruit of our ministry, He looks for the fruit of our lives. Even though we are running the race to win, the Spirit of God wants us to be temperate. God is seldom found in extremes. He instructs us to let our *"moderation be known. . . ."*[3] One fruit of the Spirit is temperance.[4]

### "So let a man examine himself . . . "

As ministering brothers and sisters, we must somehow create among ourselves a greater awareness of our need to judge ourselves. For, in this Communion passage of Scripture, we're reminded that when we do not judge ourselves, we are judged and chastened of the Lord in order that we should not be condemned with the world.

In the last three years, we have seen three prominent leaders of the church seriously wounded among us. I cannot remember another time in our denominational history when events have so tragically impacted our ranks. What can we do about that? What can I do about that? We can carefully and regularly examine our spiritual health.

God gave us a beautiful means of self-examination. Even a casual study of the New Testament church reveals that they celebrated Communion every week. And . . . part of the directive concerning Communion is, *"Let a man so examine himself."*[5] Following Communion, they brought offerings consisting of whatever they had to give. And they divided the offerings among the poor. They took care of one another. Perhaps they realized, as no other generation of Christians has, that because we are all members of one Body, what one of us does vitally affects the rest of us. When one member suffers, the whole Body suffers.

The English poet and preacher John Donne put it this way: *"No man is an island entire of itself; every man is a piece of the continent . . . when the bell tolls, ask not for whom it tolls. It tolls for thee."*[6]

Donne's message reinforces the very clear directive of Scripture that, in addition to being one with Christ, we are made one Body with each other:

*"For as the body is one, and hath many members, and all the members of that one body, being many, are one body: so*

*also is Christ . . . But now hath God set the members every one
of them in the body, as it hath pleased him . . . but now are they
many members, yet but one body . . . God hath tempered the
body together . . . now ye are the body of Christ, and members
in particular."*[7]

*"Whether we live, we live unto the Lord; or whether we die, we
die unto the Lord."*[8] The way in which we live, and the way in which we
die, affects not only our own life, but the entire body of believers to
whom we are joined in Christ.

## Learning by example

Paul reminds us in the first part of 1 Corinthians chapter 10 that
all the things that happened to Israel in the wilderness are recorded in
part for examples. They lived with the consequences of their choices.
When they chose wisely, they had good consequences. When they made
poor decisions, they lived with poor consequences. Likewise, Scriptural
accounts of the Early Church's practices are examples for our benefit.
Oh, that we might have the wisdom to learn from the examples of those
in the faith who have gone before us!

When I was a child, I used to get so tired of hearing my mother
say to me, "Now, son, if you don't listen, you'll have to feel!" Anytime
I'd play too near the stairway, or get too close to the stove, or when she
thought I wasn't looking both ways before I crossed the street, she would
repeat that warning. Insisting that she was looking out for my welfare,
she would say again, "If you don't listen, son, you'll have to feel." And
sometimes, as she applied her "board of education" to my "seat of
learning," I most certainly *felt* . . . because I hadn't *listened.*

It would be tragic indeed for the Body of Christ to suffer what
we have suffered through the past few years and not learn something
valuable from it. Those who have fallen among us are *no less a part of
us* simply because they have fallen. We may excommunicate them from
our fellowship, but we do not have the power to excommunicate them
from the Body of Christ. That is a power God reserves for himself. If
they are repentant, He will forgive and restore them. However, the Body
of Christ in its entirety is diminished in its effectiveness—and greatly
embarrassed—by their behavior.

Sometimes we see in the failure of another person what we *fear*—or perhaps secretly *know* to be true—in ourselves. When this happens, we tend to project what we can't stand about ourselves onto the person who fails. By striking out at *them*, we strike out at what we cannot stand about *ourselves*.

## Temptations are a common occurrence

May we not be so preoccupied with the failures of others this morning that we do not understand what Paul is saying directly to each of us in 1 Corinthians 10:12: *"Wherefore let him that thinketh he standeth take heed lest he fall."* Paul is urging the Corinthians to learn from the examples of the Israelites in order to be spared the pain of learning through personal experience. In his efforts to warn the Corinthians, I hear him saying three things:

First of all, he is saying that everyone is tempted. *"There hath no temptation taken you but such as is common to man."*[9] Even Jesus was tempted.[10] For us to think that we can live free of temptation is to deceive ourselves.

Everyone is tempted, and all of our temptations are common. Solomon said it centuries ago: *". . . There is no new thing new under the sun . . . Is there any thing whereof it may be said, See, this is new? it hath been already of old time, which was before us."*[11] If there's anything I have a chance to see in operation more frequently than perhaps some of you, it's how ridiculously limited the enemy's arsenal is. He employs money, sex, and spiritual pride, or sex, spiritual pride, and money, or spiritual pride, money, and sex.

If the enemy can make you think that your temptations are unique or weird, you'll want to hide them and make a secret of them rather than confess and forsake them. Once the walls of silence go up around your secret, it's only a matter of time before the walls of your life come tumbling down.

For God has not made us to hide ourselves behind walls: He has made us to *". . . walk in the light, as he is in the Light,"* so that we can *"have fellowship one with another . . ."*—with Him, with ourselves, and with other believers—having been cleansed from our sin by the *". . . blood of Jesus Christ his Son."*[12]

Everyone is tempted. That's not where we sin and fail. Sin and failure are the result of giving in to temptation; of, as a ministry colleague used to put it, "crawling away from temptation real slow in the hope that it will overtake you." We cannot flirt with temptation. That's dangerous: *"Let no man say when he is tempted, I am tempted of God: for God cannot be tempted with evil, neither tempteth he any man: But every man is tempted, when he is drawn away of his own lust, and enticed. Then when lust hath conceived, it bringeth forth sin: and sin, when it is finished, bringeth forth death. Do not err [in understanding and heeding this], my beloved brethren."*[13]

### There is a way of escape

The second thing Paul is saying in 1 Corinthians 10:13 is that nobody has to fall: *" . . . God is faithful, who will not suffer you to be tempted above that you are able."* No one has to fall. No child of God ever falls by an act of God's will. When we fall, we fall by an act of our own will . . . my will . . .your will. No one has to fall.

Someone may say, *If God doesn't tempt us beyond our ability to resist temptation, then why didn't He protect these prominent, powerful people who claimed to be working for Him? Why didn't God protect them? Wouldn't that have been better for His kingdom?* God is no respecter of persons, my friend.[14] And we are created with a free will of our own to make choices of our own—for better or for worse. If God interfered with those choices, forcing some things on us and keeping us from doing some other things, then we would not be agents of free will. We would be robots. The freedom to choose for ourselves is an all-or-nothing proposition. He chose to make us free, knowing that many among His creation would choose to reject Him, but others would invite Him into their life as Lord and be among His agents to bring our planet back under His control. This is the message of both the Old and New Testaments: we are free to choose.[15]

James reminds us, *"Blessed is the man that endureth temptation;"* in other words, the man who doesn't give in to the temptation; *"for when he is tried, he shall receive the crown of life, which the Lord hath promised to them that love him."*[16] But how do you *endure* temptation? The word *endure* means to remain firm under onslaught, without giving in to it. We *endure*, first of all, by recognizing that any one of us is capable of doing what our brethren have done who have caused us so much grief today.

Why didn't they see the way to escape? First of all, *they weren't looking for a way to escape.* The devil has a way of hooking us on his pleasure and hiding the price tag. He will never show you the price tag until after he has deceived you with the pleasure—*and the pleasure is never worth the price.*

No adulterer sees the disappointed look on their mate's face during the moments of that sexual encounter. No adulterer hears their child saying, "Not you, Daddy!" . . . "Not you, Mom!" The enemy doesn't allow you to get that close to the price. He wants to blind you with the pleasure. He can deceive us into making us think that we have found a perfect way to cover our behavior. But his solutions—like his pleasures— are counterfeit and are only temporary at best.

There is one perfect covering for our sin: it's the blood of our Lord Jesus Christ. *"He that covereth his sins shall not prosper: but who so confesseth and forsaketh them shall have mercy."*[17]  Once you start trying to cover your sins by any other means, more and more of your energy is invested in maintaining the cover, and less and less of your energy is available to live the life God has called you to live. It's impossible to deceive others until you've hidden the contents of your heart from your own self. But the more effectively you deceive yourself, the more skilled you become in deceiving others—*for a time.*

## The importance of Communion

This is why observing Communion is so important in the life of every believer. So often, pastors see it as an inconvenience that crowds the Sunday morning service. But, friends, this is what "the Sunday morning service" is all about! When you bring the people of God to a the Table of self-examination, you are engaging in one of the most important activities of the ministry.

At this Table they are reminded of Jeremiah's lament, that, *"The heart is deceitful above all things, and desperately wicked: who can know it?"*[18] And you can assure them that the Spirit of God can know their hearts, for He searches the *"deep things;"*[19] the Word of God is also quite capable of knowing their hearts: *" . . . piercing even to the*

*dividing asunder of soul and spirit . . . and is a discerner of the thoughts
and intents of the heart.*"[20] *"Search me, O God, and know my heart:
try me, and know my thoughts: And see if there be any wicked way in
me, and lead me in the way everlasting.*"[21] This was David's prayer to
the God Who described him as, *". . . a man after mine own heart, which
shall fulfil all my will.*"[22]

No one ever falls because God doesn't make a way to escape.
God *always* makes a way to escape. Joseph found it. Once Christ touched
her life, Mary Magdalene found it. Job found it. If you need a way to
escape, God will help you find one if you ask Him.

You may be here this morning tempted, tested; perhaps allowing
things to go on in the privacy and secrecy of your heart that the Holy
Spirit has been convicting you of. Friend, see the pain you are
experiencing as part of God's redemptive love for you. When my body
hurts, my brain gets control of my mind. Pain gets my attention and
makes me do whatever I can to stop it. And when any one of us gets too
far from the way God has called us to live in His Word, unless we have
seared our conscience,[23] the Holy Spirit is faithful in inflicting spiritual
pain. He lovingly chastens us in order to bring us to repentance so that
we will not be condemned with the world. He is there to keep us from
falling and to present us faultless before the throne of God.[24] And this
moment is our time for personal, private self-examination, to see what
there is in our lives that He needs to call to our attention. So, as we
approach the Lord's Table, let us remember Paul's admonition:

*" . . . Wherefore whosoever shall eat this bread, and
drink this cup of the Lord, unworthily, shall be guilty of the body
and blood of the Lord. But let a man examine himself, and so let
him eat of that bread, and drink of that cup. For he that eateth
and drinketh unworthily, eateth and drinketh damnation to
himself, not discerning the Lord's body.*"[25]

Let's listen to Paul's account of the first Communion service:

*" . . . That the Lord Jesus the same night in which he
was betrayed took bread: And when he had given thanks, he
brake it, and said, Take, eat: this is my body, which is broken for
you: this do in remembrance of me.*"[26]

Shall we eat together.

*"After the same manner also he took the cup, when he had supped, saying, This cup is the new testament in my blood: this do ye, as oft as ye drink it, in remembrance of me. For as often as ye eat this bread, and drink this cup, ye do shew the Lord's death till he come. Wherefore whosoever shall eat this bread, and drink this cup of the Lord, unworthily, shall be guilty of the body and blood of the Lord. But let a man examine himself, and so let him eat of that bread, and drink of that cup. For he that eateth and drinketh unworthily, eateth and drinketh damnation to himself, not discerning the Lord's body. For this cause many are weak and sickly among you, and many sleep. For if we would judge ourselves, we should not be judged. But when we are judged, we are chastened of the Lord, that we should not be condemned with the world.*"[27]

Let us drink together.

God wants to remind us this morning of how much we need each other—and how utterly dependent we are upon Him—to keep us from falling. May we truly *have "an ear to hear"*[28] what He would say to each of us individually, to all of us as ministers of His gospel to a lost and dying world, and to His Church.

---

[1] 1 Corinthians 9:24-10:17.
[2] 1 Corinthians 1:10; 11:18.
[3] Philippians 4:5.
[4] Galatians 5:23.
[5] 1 Corinthians 11:28.
[6] Donne, John, **Devotions Upon Emergent Occasions**, 1624.
[7] 1 Corinthians 12:12-27.
[8] Romans 14:7,8.
[9] 1 Corinthians 10:13.
[10] Matthew 4:1-10.
[11] Ecclesiastes 1:9-11.
[12] 1 John 1:7-9.
[13] James 1:13-16.
[14] Acts 10:34.

15 Joshua 24:14,15; Matthew 6:24.
16 James 1:12.
17 Proverbs 28:13.
18 Jeremiah 17:9.
19 1 Corinthians 2:10.
20 Hebrews 4:12.
21 Psalm 139:23,24.
22 Acts 13:22.
23 1 Timothy 4:2.
24 Jude, v. 24.
25 1 Corinthians 11:27-29.
26 1 Corinthians 11:23,24.
27 1 Corinthians 11:25-32.
28 Revelation 3:6; 13:9.

# 4

# Discerning the Lord's Body *

What a special time of year this is—it's the only time of the year when we as ministers and spouses of ministers, along with leaders from our various churches, can celebrate Communion together. This year, before we partake of the Lord's Supper, we're going to consider the importance of discerning His body in our observance of Communion.

> *"For I have received of the Lord that which also I delivered unto you, That the Lord Jesus the same night in which he was betrayed took bread: And when he had given thanks, he brake it, and said, Take eat: this is my body, which is broken for you: this do in remembrance of me.*

> *"After the same manner also he took the cup, when he had supped, saying, This cup is the new testament in my blood: this do ye, as oft as ye drink it, in remembrance of me. For as often as ye eat this bread, and drink this cup, ye do shew the Lord's death till he come.*

> *"Wherefore whosoever shall eat this bread, and drink this cup of the Lord, unworthily, shall be guilty of the body and blood of the Lord. But let a man examine himself, and so let him eat of that bread, and drink of that cup. For he that eateth and drinketh unworthily, eateth and drinketh damnation to himself, not discerning the Lord's body. For this cause many are weak and sickly among you, and many sleep. For if we would judge ourselves, we should not be judged. But when we are judged, we*

---

* Sermon for the Communion Service of the 1988 Ohio District Council of the Assemblies of God, Akron Springfield Assembly of God, Akron, Ohio.

*are chastened of the Lord, that we should not be condemned with the world."*[1]

### God made us for relationships

God created us to need relationships—relationships with Him and with each other. When He made Adam, He observed that *". . . it is not good that the man should be alone . . ..*[2] Adam needed a helpmate; a companion.

I believe that one of the most prominent reasons people become emotionally disturbed, mentally ill, and/or spiritually backslidden, is that we forget our need for God and we forget our need for each other. This happens in spite of the fact that God tells us it is *"not good"* to be alone.

### Don't play "Lone Ranger" in the ministry!

In the ministry, we tend to play "Lone Ranger." Often, when we think about observing Communion, we think about what we have done to offend the Lord or to offend each other. And this is good. As we examine ourselves this morning, we do need to address our sins of commission. Those thoughts and actions that separate us from God will, sooner or later, separate us from each other. So we need to ask His forgiveness for them as soon as we are aware of their existence.

We can draw close to God and still purposely keep our distance from others. However, this kind of behavior invites attacks of the enemy. His strategy is to divide us from one another and then conquer us as isolated individuals. As members of the clergy, we are especially prone to purposely isolating ourselves from close friendships. We are so competitive. We don't want anyone to know us well enough to know when our church is experiencing problems or when something is wrong in our personal life. But this can be very devastating. Each of us needs two or three close friends in whom we can confide *almost anything* without fear of rejection. We were made for relationships—with God and with fellow human beings. Far too many of us are woefully lacking in this area. So we also need to address our sins of *omission*—the things we haven't done—as we prepare to partake of Communion. And there's more.

God also wants to talk to us about discerning both *His broken body* and *those who are bruised and brokenhearted among the Body.*

## His Body . . . the Church

Communion should not only remind us of the wounded, bleeding, dying, physical body of the Lord, but it should also remind us of the bruised, bound, and brokenhearted members of our Lord's Body, the Church. When we take the cup and the bread, we should certainly think of His body triumphantly bearing the scars of our redemption in heaven. But we likewise need to think of His Body, the Church on earth, and those members who are broken, bound and bruised by life. We need to pray for this part of the Body to be strengthened and made whole so that the entire Body may benefit from having its members in good health:

> *"For as the body is one, and hath many members, and all the members of that one body, being many, are one body: so also is Christ. For by one Spirit are we all baptized into one body, whether we be Jews or Gentiles, whether we be bond or free; and have been all made to drink into one Spirit. For the body is not one member, but many.*

> *"If the foot shall say, Because I am not the hand, I am not of the body; is it therefore not of the body? And if the ear shall say, because I am not the eye, I am not of the body; is it therefore not of the body? If the whole body were an eye, where were the hearing? If the whole were hearing, where were the smelling? But now hath God set the members every one of them in the body, as it hath pleased him. And if they were all one member, where were the body? But now are they many members, yet but one body."*[3]

## We want to feel needed and unique

We are so fearful the Body will not need us. We are desirous of being unique and indispensable. And yet, the truth is that we are all dispensable. Before we meet again around the Lord's Table, only God knows how many of our names will be read among the list of those who have gone to be with Him since our last Council meeting. And . . . both the institutional church and the greater Body of Christ on earth will get along very well without us. It's not important that we be unique here. God wants us to be ourselves, of course, but He also wants us to feel our need of others in the Body.

Whenever we feel that any genuine move of the Spirit that happens in *our city* must happen in *our church,* we are being very selfish and competitive. This attitude smacks of a spiritual elitism that the Lord detests. From this perspective, if a revival breaks out somewhere else in town, it's easy to feel that it must be spurious—or, at best, superficial—when one is doing and saying all the right things and nothing is happening in *his or her church.* From this point of view, anything "real" that God does in their city will happen where *they* pastor—not across town.

### The farmer doesn't own the harvest

In the last couple of years, God has been trying to help us see that it is dangerous for the farmer to claim the harvest. He who plants is nothing. He who waters is nothing. The harvest belongs to God, and each of us has an equally important role in producing it.

> *"For, brethren, ye have been called unto liberty; only use not liberty for an occasion to the flesh, but by love serve one another. For all the law is fulfilled in one word, even in this; Thou shalt love thy neighbour as thyself. But if ye bite and devour one another [a fatal affliction of the church] take heed that ye be not consumed one of another.*

> *"This I say then, Walk in the Spirit, and ye shall not fulfil the lust of the flesh. For the flesh lusteth against the Spirit, and the Spirit against the flesh: and these are contrary the one to the other: so that ye cannot do the things that ye would. But if ye be led of the Spirit, ye are not under the law.*

> *" Now the works of the flesh are manifest, which are these: Adultery, fornication, uncleanness, lasciviousness, Idolatry, witchcraft, hatred, variance, emulations, wrath, strife, seditions, heresies, Envyings, murders, drunkenness, revellings, and such like: of the which I tell you before, as I have also told you in time past, that they which do such things shall not inherit the kingdom of God. But the fruit of the Spirit is love, joy, peace, longsuffering, gentleness, goodness, faith, Meekness, temperance: against such there is no law. "And they that are Christ's have crucified the flesh with the affections and lusts.*

> *"If we live in the Spirit, let us also walk in the Spirit. Let us not be desirous of vain glory, provoking one another,*

*envying one another. Brethren, if a man be overtaken in a fault, ye which are spiritual, restore such an one in the spirit of meekness; considering thyself, lest thou also be tempted. Bear ye one another's burdens, and so fulfill the law of Christ.*

*"For if a man thinketh himself to be something, when he is nothing, he deceiveth himself. But let every man prove his own work, and then shall he have rejoicing in himself alone, and not in another. For every man shall bear his own burden. Let him that is taught in the word communicate unto him that teacheth in all good things.*

*"Be not deceived; God is not mocked: for whatsoever a man soweth, that shall he also reap. For he that soweth to his flesh shall of the flesh reap corruption; but he that soweth to the Spirit shall of the Spirit reap life everlasting. And let us not be weary in well-doing: for in due season we shall reap, if we faint not. As we have therefore opportunity, let us do good unto all men, especially unto them who are of the household of faith."*[4]

From the beginning of this passage to the end, God is reminding us that we are members of His body. How we treat one another is a reflection of how we really feel toward Him. For when we bite and devour one another, it is not simply that we hurt one another; but we hurt Him.

Notice in particular that Paul says in this passage: *"... Do good unto all men, especially unto them who are of the household of faith."* What kind of care do we give one another? Do we truly seek opportunity to do good to those who are *"of the household of faith"*?

### Christians are to unselfishly care for each other

From my observation, friend, both the institutional church and its individual members can be very selfish. We have to take a look at our motives. Too often we are interested in people only because they are essential to our statistical success. We want to be able to include them among our membership roll; our regular, tithe-paying attenders.

What kind of care do we provoke members of our churches to take of each other? When we come to Communion, we are not only to think of what we have done *to our Lord,* but *to each other;* not only what we have done *for our Lord,* but *for each other.*

His prayer for us is that we *become one both with Him and with each other*.[5] But it is hard to feel that we are *at one* with someone toward whom we feel suspicious . . . or envious. When it strains us to find even one earthly person to whom we might confess some uncomplimentary part of our lives, we lack the love and unity to adequately present Christ to the world. How can we bring those attitudes to the Communion Table— and leave still carrying them with us—believing that we are in the will of God and "one" with Him?

### Binding each other and and setting each other free

Matthew 18:15-20 is often quoted as a passage that gives believers the right to collaborate with one another to get what they want from God. But is that really what this passage says? Let's read it together and find out:

> *"Moreover if thy brother shall trespass against thee, go and tell him his fault between thee and him alone: if he shall hear thee, thou hast gained thy brother. But if he will not hear thee, then take with thee one or two more, that in the mouth of two or three witnesses, every word may be established. And if he shall neglect to hear them, tell it unto the church: but if he neglect to hear the church, let him be unto thee as an heathen man and a publican.*

> *"Verily I say unto you, Whatsoever ye shall bind on earth shall be bound  in heaven: and whatsoever ye shall loose on earth shall be loosed in heaven. Again I say unto you, That if two of you shall agree on earth as touching any thing that they shall ask, it shall be done for them of my Father which is in Heaven. For where two or three are gathered together in my name, there am I in the midst of them."*[6]

Notice, Matthew didn't pick up on the instrumental opportunity of using agreement to get something for himself. He went right to his relationships. And he said, *"Lord, how oft shall my brother sin against me, and I forgive him? till seven times? Jesus saith unto him, I say not unto thee, Until seven times: but, Until seventy times seven."*[7] The parable that follows this passage is about the rich man who forgave a servant's large debt. But *that same servant* would not extend compassion to a fellow servant who owed *him* a much lesser amount. Not only did he not forgive him the debt—he went out looking for him and grabbed him around the throat while he was making his point!

The point *I'm* making, my friends, is this: many of the people I see in my office would never need to be there if they had one or two wholesome Christian friends with whom they could confess their faults one to another and pray one for another. Many ministers eventually end up in my office because they feel so isolated and alone. They are very aware of their sins—and terrified that someone will find out and report them.

The vast majority of these ministers are hardworking people who love the ministry and love the Lord. Most are not guilty of things that would require them to surrender their credentials. Most often, the worst thing they have done is to try to go it alone. They are guilty of not reaching out and recognizing their need for other members of the Body of Christ.

In terms of the vertical dimension of their faith, they're ready for heaven. But in terms of the horizontal dimension of their faith, they're lonely, isolated, angry, suspicious, depressed, and scared. Who has bound them like that? We—their brothers and sisters—have bound them like that. For there is a sense in which I can bind you, and a sense in which I can also set you free—simply in the way I choose to relate to you and the way in which I encourage you to relate to me. I believe this is the real message of Matthew 18:15-20.

### Creating a community of love and forgiveness

We are about to approach the Lord's Table. I ask you to discern in the bread and the cup the price Jesus paid to set us free from our sins so that we no longer need to fear God's wrath. May I also ask you to discern in these elements the price Jesus paid so that we could feel secure in His love . . . and secure in our love for one another as members of His Body?

I ask you this morning to pledge yourself—along with me—to create the kind of loving community that will allow us to, " . . . *walk in the light, as he is in the light, [so that] we have fellowship with one another, and the blood of Jesus Christ his Son [may cleanse] us from all sin.* "[8] I ask you to join me in praying that God will deliver us from the deception that we are without sin. For, *"If we say that we have no sin, we deceive ourselves, and the truth is not in us.*"[9] Instead of denying our sins, may we be transparent enough to confess them to God so that He may demonstrate to us, as often as needed, that He is, *" . . . faithful and just to forgive us our sins, and cleanse us from all unrighteousness."*[10]

Then, having confessed our sins to God and having received His forgiveness, let us reach out to one another, to *"Bear . . . one another's burdens, and so fulfill the law of Christ."*[11] We need to extend to those who have trespassed against us that same forgiveness we receive for our own trespasses when we come to the Table of the Lord. We need to love them and set them free to serve God in a totally loving, forgiven state.

We've already talked about Paul's admonition to the church, to, *" . . . let a man examine himself, and so let him eat of that bread, and drink of that cup."* May the Lord remind us what our sins did to His body . . . and what our sins are still doing to His Body on earth, the Church. May He help us to fulfill His prayer for us that we may *be one* even as He, the Father, and the Holy Spirit are one. May we set each other loose in the love of God by forgiving those who have trespassed against us. May we rise above our tendency to gossip about those who have fallen. May we consider our own sinful nature, lest we also give in to temptation.

If this last year has taught me anything, it is that I not only need His physical body, I need His Body as represented by my brothers and sisters on earth. Pinnacles of success are treacherous places for us. They tempt us to forget how dependent we are on Christ and how much we need each other. Success in the ministry can breed an arrogance and elitism that puts us at risk for tragedy. What we have seen in recent months should make this plain to all of us.

I need the Body of Christ more than they need me. My physical body is temporal; it is tied to this world of time and space. My body may not last until Christ's return. However, the Church will survive until that day. As long as you and I survive, we need that Body to help nourish and protect our spiritual welfare.

### Enlarge your circle of friends

Allow God to enlarge your circle of friends. Let's be careful that we don't leave people out. One of the times loneliness is felt most intensely is when one is alone in a crowd of people where others all seem to be with someone who knows them and enjoys their company. Let's include others in our circle of fellowship during this Council. May God help us to take from this Table a greater sense of responsibility for our fellow minister; our fellow minister's spouse. May He help us remember to write; to call; to pray; to express some kindness to those in need. May God deliver us from feeling that when we have paid our taxes we've discharged our obligation to the poor; or that when we have given to missions we have done our part to win the world to Jesus.

We need the human contact that *giving alms* provides. We need the contact of *bearing one another's burdens*. We need the contact of *sharing the love of Christ with others*. May God remind us today and every time we approach His Table that our focus should be not only on the broken physical body of the Lord, but also on our relationships with other members of the Body of Christ on earth. These need to be examined as well.

If we truly discern the Lord's Body, I believe that great healing, great liberation, great forgiveness, great strength, and great unity can come to the Church. But that process will be in direct proportion to our ability to *become one* with Him and our brothers and sisters in Christ at the Table of the Lord—and *remain one* after we leave.

Shall we bow our hearts in prayer.

*When we partake of Communion, Lord, we often think of Your broken body, thorn-pierced brow, pierced side, and nail-scarred hands and feet. And it is right that we should—because You paid such a terrible price for us. And until we first discern the importance of Your sacrifice and get ourselves in a right relationship with You, we can go no farther in our relationships with others. Beyond that, God, help us see what our thoughtlessness does to each other. Help us see what our carelessness does to each other. Help us to see that this kind of behavior toward others helps further the enemy's kingdom, not Yours, because when he divides the unity of the Church, he neutralizes the power of the Church.*

*You already know, Lord, how very much each of us wants to feel loved. How much each of us wants to feel needed. How each of us is so often tempted to feel insecure. You know how easy it is for us to feel unnoticed and unappreciated. Help us to realize when we have done this to one another, Lord, so that we may seek forgiveness. Help us reach out to each other in largeness of heart. Help us, Oh God, to be generous in spirit.*

*Let the fruit of the Spirit be born in us, Lord—not just that we may please You and draw near to You, but so that love, joy, peace, meekness, gentleness, goodness, faith, and temperance*[12] *may bind us to each other. Oh God, deliver us from thinking just of the vertical dimension of our faith. What good does it do to draw close to You if we don't use Your touch upon our lives to draw close to each other? We need each other, Lord. You made us to need each other, just as You made us to need You.*

*As we discern Your Body in the bread and Your blood in the cup, Lord, help us to understand that one of the things we can do that will most gladden Your heart is to open our hearts to each other. This is how You said others would know that we are Your disciples.*[13] *So not only make us one with You, Lord Jesus, but also help us tear down the walls between us and spread tables of love and forgiveness for each other after the manner in which You spread such a Table before each of us.*

*Take us back to our churches looking for opportunities to sincerely do good. We know, Lord, that it is when others see our good works—things we don't have the strength of will to do on our own, but can only do as You empower us—that they will glorify our Father Who is in heaven. When others see Your unselfishness reflected in the unselfishness of our lives, in our willingness to give to those who can't give back, they will want to know the Source of that kind of lifestyle. This is how we will win the world for You . . . and how we will love our brothers and sisters in Christ and give ourselves for them even as You gave Yourself for us—*"Not with eye-service, as men-pleasers; but as the servants of Christ, doing the will of God from the heart; With good will doing service, as to the Lord, and not to men."[14] *Help us "do good" in this way—*toward our fellow believers and unbelievers alike, *but* to You. *Help us do it for* their benefit *and for* Your glory, *not for our own.*

*Speak to us this morning about someone among our acquaintances who needs a letter, a phone call, a gift of money; someone who may need help managing an overwhelming responsibility in their family. Oh God, may we discern both Your broken physical body and the*

*Body of Christ here on earth in the bread and the cup, so that we may become one with You and with each other. In Jesus' Name we pray, Amen.*

---

[1] 1 Corinthians 11:23-32.
[2] Genesis 2:18.
[3] 1 Corinthians 12:12-20.
[4] Galatians 5:13-6:10.
[5] John 17:11,21-26.
[6] Matthew 18:15-20.
[7] Matthew 18:21, 22.
[8] 1 John 1:7.
[9] 1 John 1:8.
[10] 1 John 1:9.
[11] Galatians 6:2.
[12] Galatians 5:22,23.
[13] John 13:35.
[14] Ephesians 6:6,7.

# 5

# Symbols of a Caring Church *

*"Now before the feast of the passover, when Jesus knew that his hour was come that he should depart out of this world unto the Father, having loved his own which were in the world, he loved them unto the end. And supper being ended, the devil having now put into the heart of Judas Iscariot, Simon's son, to betray him; Jesus knowing that the Father had given all things into his hands, and that He was come from God, and went to God; He riseth from supper, and laid aside His garments; and took a towel, and girded himself. After that he poureth water into a basin, and began to wash the disciples' feet, and to wipe them with the towel wherewith He was girded.*

*"Then cometh he to Simon Peter: and Peter saith unto him, Lord, dost thou wash my feet? Jesus answered and said unto him, What I do thou knowest not now; but thou shalt know hereafter. Peter saith unto him, Thou shalt never wash my feet. Jesus answered him, If I wash thee not, thou hast no part with me. Simon Peter saith unto him, Lord, not my feet only, but also my hands and my head.*

*"Jesus saith to him, He that is washed needeth not save to wash his feet, but is clean every whit: and ye are clean, but not all. For he knew who should betray him; therefore said he, Ye are not all clean.*

*So after he had washed their feet, and had taken his garments, and was set down again, he said unto them, Know ye*

*Sermon for the Communion Service of the 1989 Ohio District Council of the Assemblies of God, Evangel Assembly of God, Columbus, Ohio.

*what I have done to you? Ye call me Master and Lord: and ye say well; for so I am. If I then, your Lord and Master, have washed your feet; ye also ought to wash one another's feet. For I have given you an example, that ye should do as I have done to you. Verily, verily, I say unto you, The servant is not greater than his lord; neither he that is sent greater than he that sent him. If ye know these things, happy are ye if ye do them."*[1]

Those words are from the Gospel of John. Now let's turn to Peter's first letter to the believers who have fled Asia Minor, encouraging them to trust in God:

*"The elders which are among you I exhort, who am also an elder, and a witness of the sufferings of Christ, and also a partaker of the glory that shall be revealed: Feed the flock of God which is among you, taking the oversight thereof, not by constraint, but willingly; not for filthy lucre, but of a ready mind; Neither as being lords over God's heritage, but being ensamples to the flock.*

*"And when the chief Shepherd shall appear, ye shall receive a crown of glory that fadeth not away. Likewise, ye younger, submit yourselves unto the elder. Yea, all of you be subject one to another, and be clothed with humility: for God resisteth the proud, and giveth grace to the humble. Humble yourselves therefore under the mighty hand of God, that he may exalt you in due time: Casting all your care upon Him; for He careth for you."*[2]

Now let's go back to the Gospel of John for two final verses:

*"Verily, verily, I say unto you, Except a corn of wheat fall into the ground and die, it abideth alone: but if it die, it bringeth forth much fruit. He that loveth his life shall lose it; and he that hateth his life in this world shall keep it until life eternal."*[3]

Shall we bow our hearts in prayer.

*Father, we thank You for those who have gone before us. It is into a continuation of their labors that we have now entered, for none of us lives to himself or dies to himself. We are members of Your Body,*

*totally dependent upon You, our blessed Lord, as the Head of that Body,
and interdependent upon each other. As we approach Your Table this
morning, let us examine ourselves. Search us, Lord. See the resentment
that is there because we feel others have not cared enough for us. Show
us our need to be so lost in caring for others that there's no room in our
hearts to resent others' lack of care for us. In Jesus' Name we pray,
Amen.*

The impact the church is making on the American culture today
is not nearly as great as *the impact the American culture is making on
the church.* We are often too engrossed in the burdens of our work and
the cares of life to see what is happening. But if we can detach ourselves
enough to look around objectively, we will clearly see that the church is
becoming more "American" instead of influencing our nation into
becoming more "Christian."

### A contrast in generations

The change in the secular entertainment industry is an
unmistakable sign of the direction in which we are moving. Back when
many of us were growing up, the popular television shows (for those
few families who had invested in a television!) were "The Lone Ranger,"
"I Love Lucy," "My Little Margie," and "Ozzie and Harriet." Today, it's
"Eight is Enough," "Three's Company," "Falcon Crest," and "Dallas."
This reflects a gigantic shift in cultural values in just one generation.

During this same period of time, the American church has
become much more materialistic than it has ever been. Being *a child of
the King* means something very different today than in past generations.
People of faith are identified nowadays by their wealth and luxurious
lifestyle. Don't misunderstand me, please—the up-and-outers are just
as much in need of Christ as the down-and-outers. The church has always
had its wealthy members, such as Lydia, Barnabas, the family of Lazarus,
and others. However, many voices in the church today are telling us that
the absence of wealth (or good health) reflects a lack of faith. These
people would have us believe that God wants all of His children to be
both healthy and wealthy.

Those of us who grew up a few years back also believed we
were *King's Kids,* but our focus was different from that of today's yuppie
Christianity.  Because we were King's Kids, we downplayed the

importance of wealth in this world. Our riches were in heaven and were more valuable than earthly, material wealth.

We sang—and believed with all our heart—

*"A tent or a cottage, why should I care?*
*They're building a mansion for me over there."*

We didn't have to have much in this world; our reward would come in the next one. Today's generation of the church says, in marked contrast, Because I am a King's Kid, nothing is too good for me in the sweet here-and-now.

### The selfishness of the world spills over into the Church

The world we live in is very selfish and greedy, and God's people are affected by these qualities of the people among whom they live and work. Prime evidence of how this affects us is found in the extent to which we are *more aware of those times when we have been neglected by others* than we are of *opportunities we have for serving others.* The church desperately needs us to be *servant leaders.*

Our churches are not going to be full of people who unselfishly care for others unless we as their pastors and church leaders unselfishly care for *them.* Jesus modeled servant leadership for His disciples at the Last Supper and identified this kind of leadership as the way for His followers to be happy doing His work: *"If ye know these things, happy are ye if ye do them."*[4]

### Look for opportunities to serve

As we partake of the emblems of the Lord's broken body and His shed blood this morning, let us examine ourselves in this regard. I am not suggesting that we condemn ourselves for serving others too seldom—there is no way we can go back and reclaim the opportunities we have missed and there is certainly enough other ammunition for self-condemnation. However, I *am* asking that we seek God's help in becoming more alert to future opportunities to care for others—and especially our ministry friends. We cannot afford to ignore each other's needs.

Remember, Jesus said this is one way the world would recognize that His followers are different; that they care for each other's needs:

*"By this shall all men know that ye are my disciples, if ye have love one to another."*[5] Paul amplifies this directive for us: *"And be ye kind one to another, tenderhearted, forgiving one another, even as God for Christ's sake has forgiven you."*[6] In Galatians he says very much the same thing in another way: *"For all the law is fulfilled in one word, even in this; Thou shalt love thy neighbor as thyself."*[7] Also in Galatians, he reminds us that our witness should extend beyond the Christian community: *"As we have therefore opportunity, let us do good unto all men, especially unto them who are of the household of faith."*[8]

It is natural to want someone to care for you. And *wanting to care for others* should be a natural outgrowth of spiritual maturity. If people are to learn this unselfish way of loving, then we, as servant leaders, must model it for them. This modeling is what Peter is referring to when he admonishes the elders of the church: *"Feed the flock of God which is among you, taking the oversight thereof . . . Neither as being lords over God's heritage, but being ensamples to the flock."*[9]

**The crown and the scepter . . . or the basin and the towel?**

Let us refuse to adopt the worldly symbols of power and prosperity—the scepter and the crown—for our symbols. There will be plenty of time for that when we stand in the presence of the Lord if we have been true to Him on earth. He will reward us when He welcomes us home. Until we get there, let's take up the basin and the towel, for, *"If ye know these things, happy are ye if ye do them."* We may infer from Christ's foregoing statement that if we do not take up the basin and the towel—if we do not *lead by following* through the practice of servant leadership—we will be less happy and less fulfilled in our ministry. I suspect that all of us would rather try to follow His example than chart our own ministry methods—He has already given us the formula.

Let us ask the Lord to peel the calluses from our hearts and make us tender before Him. Let us ask Him to give us eyes to see those on the other side of the road who are in trouble and have fallen among forces that are bent on their destruction. As we take the emblems of Communion in our hands this morning, may we realize that His heart is broken for the needs of this world. I pray we will not consume this bread thinking only of ourselves. Instead, may we take a lesson from the Israelite family that was too small to consume an entire Passover lamb and so brought in others to share it with them. May we diligently seek opportunities to share the life-giving provisions the Lamb of God has made for us.

Shall we bow our hearts in prayer.

*Our Father, as we prepare ourselves for Communion today, I pray that You will give us caring hearts. Oh God, so often when we hurt and there's no one there to care for us, it's easy for us to become so preoccupied with our own pain and loneliness that we neglect the ministry of caring for others. Instead of becoming happy, then, we become even more sad and discouraged. Lord, I pray that as we partake of Communion this morning we will think of Your example.*

*Make the symbols of our lives the basin and the towel—not the crown and the scepter. Help us to resist the enemy's temptation to focus on those things which are so temporary and fleeting. Yes, we are children of the King, but You've sent us to be Your hand extended to others; servants to people who are lost in the darkness. As we partake of Communion this morning, Lord, help us consecrate our lives to You anew. Make our hands Your hands, extending Your love to a lost and dying world. This is our prayer this morning. In Jesus' Name, Amen.*

Shall we eat together.

*Lord, we take the cup today and we thank You for it. Oh, God, You know our daily need of cleansing in the blood of Your only Son. And Lord, You know,* "if we say that we have no sin, we deceive ourselves, and the truth is not in us."[10] *Spare us, Lord, the prayer of the Pharisee; and give us the heart of the publican who* " . . . smote upon his breast, saying, God be merciful to me a sinner."[11] *Help us to be transparent before You this morning—for we know that,* " . . . if we walk in the light, as [you] are in the light, we have fellowship one with another . . . ."[12] *We know that you will be* "faithful and just to forgive us our sins and to cleanse us from all unrighteousness"[13] *when we honestly confess our sins to You.*

*Lord, help me take an honest look at my own heart and life and spend more of my energy on behalf of those who are downtrodden. How easy it is for us to think first of ourselves; how natural it is to turn away from those who need us—and need You—this morning. I pray that You will forgive us for our selfishness. Oh, God, forgive every sin that we honestly bring to You in this moment of privacy today.*

*As we drink this cup together, may it be a meaningful act of faith in Your atoning blood spilled for us. Make this a moment when the weight of our sin rolls off our lives and we become free to serve You; free to serve others. Make us aware that we are free to walk in Your Spirit, secure in the knowledge that,* "There is therefore now no condemnation to them which are in Christ Jesus, who walk not after the flesh, but after the Spirit.*"[14] We celebrate the cleansing power of Your blood this morning, Lord. Help us* "shew the Lord's death till he come."[15] *Amen.*

Shall we drink together.

---

[1] John 13:1-17
[2] 1 Peter 5:1-7.
[3] John 12:24,25.
[4] John 13:17.
[5] John 13:35.
[6] Ephesians 4:32.
[7] Galatians 5:14.
[8] Galatians 6:10.
[9] 1 Peter 5:1-3.
[10] 1 John 1:8.
[11] Luke 18:13.
[12] 1 John 1:7.
[13] 1 John 1:9.
[14] Romans 8:1.
[15] 1 Corinthians 11:26.

# 6

# Reflections on the Body and Presence of the Lord *

*"But in giving this instruction, I do not praise you, because you come together not for the better but for the worse. For, in the first place, when you come together as a church, I hear that divisions exist among you; and in part, I believe it. For there must also be factions among you, in order that those who are approved may have become evident among you.*

*"Therefore when you meet together, it is not to eat the Lord's Supper, for in your eating each one takes his own supper first; and one is hungry and another is drunk. What! Do you not have houses in which to eat and drink? Or do you despise the church of God, and shame those who have nothing? What shall I say to you? Shall I praise you? In this I will not praise you.*

*"For I received from the Lord that which also I delivered to you, that the Lord Jesus in the night in which He was betrayed took bread; and when He had given thanks, He broke it, and said, 'This is My body, which is for you; do this in remembrance of Me.'*

*"In the same way He took the cup also, after supper, saying, 'This cup is the new covenant in My blood; do this, as often as you drink it, in remembrance of Me.' For as often as you eat this bread and drink the cup, you proclaim the Lord's death until He comes.*

---

\* Sermon for the Communion Service of the 1990 Ohio District Council of the Assemblies of God, Montgomery Assembly of God, Cincinnati, Ohio.

*"Therefore whoever eats the bread or drinks the cup of the Lord in an unworthy manner, shall be guilty of the body and the blood of the Lord. But let a man examine himself, and so let him eat of the bread and drink of the cup. For he who eats and drinks, eats and drinks judgment to himself, if he does not judge the body rightly.*

*"For this reason many among you are weak and sick, and a number sleep. But if we judged ourselves rightly, we should not be judged. But when we are judged, we are disciplined by the Lord in order that we may not be condemned along with the world. So then, my brethren, when you come together to eat, wait one for another."*[1]

Shall we bow our hearts in prayer.

*Father, we can't even begin to understand the mystery of grace that calls us as strangers into a relationship even more intimate than that into which we are born by blood or joined in marriage. But when we are called by Your grace to be members of the Body of Christ, no longer are we our own. We belong to You. By right of Creation, we are Yours. By right of redemption, we are Yours. And we belong to each other, for we are members one of another.*

*This morning, as we gather at Your Table, we ask You to help us judge the Body rightly. Help us, as members of Your Body, to experience every impact You intended Your redemptive sacrifice to make in our lives. Help us rightly discern the Lord's Body in what we do. These things we pray in Jesus' Name, Amen.*

Paul draws attention to the fact that many Corinthian believers were weak and sickly, and many had even *died,* because they had not properly judged or discerned the Lord's Body in the bread and cup of Communion. What did He mean by *not properly discerning the Lord's Body?* First of all, this passage suggests that *the Corinthians had not properly judged the purpose of Christ becoming human.* However, this may have been due less to their unwillingness than to their cultural predisposition to a whole different idea about "religion." It is difficult for most people to forget their "old ways" immediately upon conversion— that's why conversion is best seen as both an instantaneous act *and* a process over time. And the greater the difference between the old and new way, the longer the time that may be required to really internalize one's new beliefs.

## Christianity is often a whole new way of life

When Paul took the message of the gospel to the Greek and Roman world, he faced the tremendous challenge of presenting not only the gospel of Jesus Christ, but a whole new approach to religious life. For, not only did the Greeks and Romans worship great numbers of gods specific to various areas of life; their gods were of a somewhat capricious nature and could not be counted on to protect suppliants no matter how great their sacrifice or how fervent their worship.

Temple worship of the gods often involved ritual prostitution with fellow worshippers and priestly prostitutes of both sexes. This was particularly common in temples built to Aphrodite—and she had many followers in Corinth. The goddess of both sacred and profane love, of marriage and harlotry, of lust and love, Aphrodite sent very mixed messages. She would capriciously lead women into adultery while encouraging them to be chaste at the same time.

Apollo, god of reason and prophecy, also had many followers and a very large temple in Corinth. Apollo was believed to be able to tell the future. His priestly *oracle*, or spokesperson, however, most often answered questions with riddles or more questions—giving such obscure responses that people could draw any number of conclusions from what the oracle said.

It is no wonder that Corinth's new converts to the Christian religion had trouble with the Christian belief in one God—especially One Who would leave His celestial home to became human so that people could understand Him. Their gods didn't do such things. They were more like a horde of squabbling brothers and sisters who dallied with human lives and emotions for their own amusement.

No doubt the Corinthian believers also found it difficult to believe that the Christian God would sacrifice His own physical body to the tremendously destructive power of sin on their behalf. Their gods demanded that sacrifices be *made to them*—they didn't sacrifice themselves *for* anyone. Their religious traditions, furthermore, focused on public processions and prayers and sacrifices—the gods could best be placated by this kind of dutiful civic observance. *How one privately felt about the gods was of little consequence as long as the public observances were kept.* There was no sacred book. There was no single, absolute, religious authority.

Beyond this conglomeration of religious ritual, Corinth was also one of the ancient world's most wealthy and worldly wise cities—a commercial seaport visited by sailing ships from all over the known world, disseminating not only their material goods but their lifestyles and *religious belief systems* among the city's inhabitants.

Thus, for the Corinthian believers, a wide variety of pagan beliefs had to be overcome by exposure to the Word of God and the testimony of the changed lives of believers *over a period of time.* In some ways, we are like the early Corinthian believers. To properly discern the Lord's body during our observance of Communion, some of our own inaccurate beliefs must be discarded and replaced with truths from God's Word. Let's look again at the biblical account of when and why God determined to send His Son to earth to redeem us to himself—and what we need to discern from that in the bread and cup each time we observe Communion.

### God needs agents of redemption on earth

At the time of Adam's creation, God was not pleased with the state of affairs on this planet. Earth was the throne of Lucifer, who was in rebellion against God.[2] God longed for His own presence to be re-established on earth. He was determined to bring this planet back under His sovereign rule. For that purpose, He created Adam from the dust of the earth. God breathed His own breath into Adam's body, and Adam sprang to life.[3]

We know the tragic story of the fall, that moment in time when Lucifer led Adam and Eve into temptation. He turned the very process by which God intended to replenish the earth with *agents of redemption* into a process that instead replenished the earth with *agents of rebellion.*[4]

Remember, God's command to Adam was, *"Be fruitful, and multiply, and replenish the earth, and subdue it: and have dominion over . . . every living thing that moveth upon the earth."*[5] But Satan struck before Adam could produce *even one unfallen offspring* who—by nature—would be obedient to God. From that moment on, the children of the *first Adam* have rebelled against presenting their bodies to God for His dwelling place.

This is why I am more and more convinced that there is no human way to improve the condition of mankind. By nature, the mind of every human being is in a state of spiritual blindness. By nature, the human will is in a state of spiritual rebellion. And so the *second Adam* came to provide God what the first Adam denied Him: a means of manifesting His presence on earth.

### "The mystery of godliness"

First, if we are going to properly discern the physical body of Christ, we must acknowledge that there is a *mystery of presence* that the human form of Christ manifested on earth. Christ's earthly body was created to visibly manifest the fullness of the power of the Godhead.[6]

In his first letter to Timothy, Paul says it is the *"mystery of godliness,"* that God was *"manifest in the flesh."*[7] And if we are going to properly discern the Lord's physical body, one of the first things we must see in the Communion emblems is that the Creator of heaven and earth has an endless and indescribable love for mankind: *"Greater love hath no man than this, that a man lay down his life for his friends."*[8] *"But God commendeth His love toward us, in that, while we were yet sinners, Christ died for us."*[9]

### Alone, we are no match for the power of sin

Second, if we are going to properly discern the purpose of Christ becoming human, we must see—in His life on earth and what finally happened to that human body—the tremendous power of sin. You and I need to understand that the god of this world possesses a power so devastating to the sons of Adam that we are no match for him. We need to remember that when the Son of God came to redeem us, the tremendous power of sin literally tore His earthly body apart. Of course, Christ reminds us that He allowed it to happen to himself: *" . . . I lay down my life, that I might take it again. No man taketh it from me, but I lay it down of myself. I have power to lay it down, and I have power to take it again. This commandment have I received of my Father."*[10] However, even though it was with Jesus' permission, the fact remains that the power of sin was strong enough to destroy His earthly body.

When we hold the emblems this morning, we are not holding reminders of the *resurrected* Christ. We are holding emblems He intended to remind us of His *death* until He comes back for His Church some day: *"This is my body, which is broken for you."*[11] *"This cup is the new testament in my blood, which is shed for you."*[12] We are holding emblems that speak of the dreadful power of sin: a power so great that when the earthly body of the son of God was offered as a willing sacrifice for our sins, it literally tore that body apart.

If I have one great fear for our fellowship, it is that we will follow the example of every other denomination before us and lose both our *respect for the power of sin* and our *acknowledged dependence on the crucified Christ to gain victory over sin.* This is a danger we face *corporately* as part of the institutional church, and *personally* as believers when we grow careless in our walk with the Lord. Not one of us is as wise or as strong as Satan.

I don't want to raise any awe or reverence for Satan. That is not my intent here. However, it is hard not to think about these things when *so many men and women of God are bringing disgrace to the Body by their careless behavior.* We must guard against becoming careless in our dependence on Christ or careless in our respect for the fearsome power of sin. I cannot keep myself free from the power of sin in my own strength. Neither can you. We need to see, in the example of what happened to the earthly body of our Lord, the awesome, fearsome power of sin and our utter dependence on Christ to keep us free of it.

We're so prone to think we can see sin coming at us; we practice by pointing at the "mote" in our brother's eye. But when we lose our dependence on the Son of God, we are so blinded by the god of this world and the "beam" he places in our own eyes that we don't even see him coming.[13] We need to see the fearsome power of sin in the broken body and shed blood of our Lord. We also need—even more—to see the awesome love and power of the God Who cared so much for us that He sent His only Son to die in our place. We need to *properly discern* the Lord's Body and blood in the bread and the cup.

Paul went so far as to suggest that many believers of his day were weak and sickly and some had even gone from this world prematurely because the bread and cup had become meaningless rituals for them. Their observance of Communion had become rote and routine. This opportunity to remember and celebrate what Christ had done for them had instead become merely an occasion for social interaction with other believers. They no longer *properly discerned* the Lord's Body.

### Temples of the Holy Spirit

The third reason Christ became human was to help us develop an awareness of our place in His plan for redeeming the world. By becoming human and using the example of the human body as His temple, He could show himself to us in a way our finite human minds could more easily understand.

The Christians of ancient Corinth had trouble grasping the divine purpose of the body as a temple of the Holy Spirit, designed to house and exhibit God's presence to unbelievers on earth. This was a foreign concept to them, remember. Their gods had no plans to redeem the world or save lost souls from destruction. So, not only did the Corinthian believers improperly judge the two reasons Christ became human in the first place, but also they were forever forgetting why God made them body persons. Three different times, in Paul's letters to the Corinthian church, he had to remind them of the spiritual purpose of their earthly body.

He makes one rather lengthy statement on the theology of the body in 1 Corinthians 6:13-7:5. And as Paul makes the transition from our relationship with God to our relationship with each other in Christian marriage, he pauses to express astonishment:

> *"What? know ye not that your body is the temple of the Holy Ghost which is in you, which ye have of God, and ye are not your own? For ye are bought with a price: therefore glorify God in your body, and in your spirit, which are God's."*[14]

Earlier in that same letter, in 1 Corinthians 3:16,17, Paul says that each of us is the temple of God and if we defile the temple, God will destroy us. In his second letter to the Corinthian church, Paul reassures those believers that if they will set themselves apart as temples of God, He will walk among them and dwell within them. He will be their Father and they will be His sons and daughters. Together they will make up the greater Body of Christ on earth. Remember, this would have been a whole new concept to the Corinthians, because their pagan gods would never have done such a thing. It's no wonder Paul's converts had such trouble internalizing this truth of Scripture. When we come to the Lord's table, we need to properly discern our bodies as members of His Body.

### We are becoming more of "stuff" than of "Spirit"

Much like the ancient Corinthians and their idol worship, the people of God in this country are trying to fill their *personal temples of God* with idols. They are no longer discerning what it means to be members of the Body. We tend to think of *idols* as belonging to other cultures; as Buddhas and jujus and totem poles. But I suggest to you this morning that believers across our nation and within our own constituency are replacing *the presence of God* with *stuff*. We no longer know the difference between luxury and necessity when it comes to material goods. We are exchanging the time we have in such limited amounts, the energy we have in limited amounts—exchanging ourselves—in the marketplaces of this world for material things rather than investing ourselves in each other and in the kingdom of God. We are composed more of *stuff* than of *spirit* at the close of the 20th century.

We are not judging our bodies properly if we judge them to be anything less than the temple of God. And we are demonstrating spiritual ignorance if we think that this temple can be satisfied with the gods of this world. For many of us, looking back upon the "good old days" of our spiritual lives doesn't produce any great longing to go back there. I can remember hearing 1 John 2:15-17 preached in a way that meant everything that was fun, fattening, or expensive was sin; but, if you could deny yourself all of those sinful pleasures while you were on earth, you would have had enough hell and you deserved to go to heaven. Most of us remember it well enough to quote it:

> *"Love not the world, neither the things that are in the world. If any man love the world, the love of the Father is not in him. For all that is in the world, the lust of the flesh, and the lust of the eyes, and the pride of life, is not of the Father, but is of the world. And the world passeth away, and the lust thereof: but he that doeth the will of God abideth forever."*

I've lived long enough now to make another observation from 1 John 2:15-17. I now see that passage saying to me, "Don't fall in love with what you have to leave." Properly discern the Lord's Body, for your body is the Lord's Body, and the Lord's Body is your body. Don't settle for a life of merely *accumulating stuff* when He's created you capable of manifesting His presence in this world.

Finally, the Corinthian Christians were apparently unable to understand the vital nature of their relationship with each other. Their celebration of the agape feast and the Lord's Supper which traditionally followed it had deteriorated so much it was no longer a time of unity and harmony. It had become an occasion that emphasized just how divided they really were. No doubt the enemy loved that; he knows he doesn't have to fear a *big* Church; he only has to fear a *united* Church.

Likewise, in this *decade of harvest*, our own human spirits and our abilities to stay united are going to be put to the test. Some among us will be given opportunities that others will not be given. Some of our fellowship will be given recognition that others will not receive; and we will all be tempted to give vent to a "Corinthian" spirit in not properly discerning the Lord's Body.

## This world needs the presence of God

With all of that in mind, I want to speak for just a moment or two before we observe Communion about what I believe is one of the most important thoughts in this passage: God created the human body because He wanted a presence in this world—a presence that Adam denied Him; a presence that Christ provided Him. If our fellowship's *decade of harvest* becomes only a mammoth church-building program, it may glorify man but it will break the heart of God. God doesn't want more buildings called churches; He wants more living temples in which He can move and live and have His being.[15] And while programs and building campaigns are excellent tools—and we must have tools if we're to be effective workmen—they're not the end product. *More living temples to house the presence of God* are the end product.

I find myself praying again and again, *"Oh, God, my generation had its Pentecost; my parents had their Pentecost. Give my sons and daughters, my grandsons and my granddaughters, their Pentecost."* Why do we need another Pentecost? Unless God breathes His presence into the body, the body is failing the very purpose for which it was created.

Please hear me out this morning. There's a longing in my heart to see us turn our church services around, because they're primarily for the people of God. I do not believe in the *burning bush* theory of evangelism. I do not believe you can set the people of a church on fire—in a world in which there are as many distractions as our world has today—and have people come rushing to see that bush that's on fire. Rather, I believe we have to set God's people on fire with His love and send them out where the unbelievers are. The church building is not God's temple. The *people who worship there* are temples of God.

### The purpose of the body

Now let's take a look at what the altar service did for us. I long for a restoration of the altar service for the people of God. There is an obvious link between a person's *body* and their *presence*. God's *purpose* for the body is to manifest the *presence of the person*. It doesn't make any difference who you are or how unaware you may be of it, whenever you enter a room you bring a presence with you. The nature of the presence you bring is determined by the spirit being who dominates your thoughts, your fantasies, and your ideas.

When many of us were growing up, our churches encouraged lengthy times of prayer around the altar following the preaching of the Word. A man or woman of God exuded a presence of God as they prayed with others at that altar. God's presence just *radiated* from them. I remember thinking, as I was praying at the altar, *Oh, God, just let the pastor come and pray behind me. I know You're here. But there's something about Your presence that becomes more intimate; more real; more intense; when the pastor is praying behind me.* Or . . . *Oh, God, don't let the evangelist spend all the time at the other end of the altar. Let him come over and pray behind me. There's something about* his *presence that intensifies* Your *presence.*

This may seem strange or mystical to you, but for me, this is the uniqueness of Pentecost. *We are people of the Presence.*

I know God is everywhere. But at those times when a man or woman of God for whom I had respect would just touch me, lay their hand on me, and pray for me, there accompanied that touch, that laying-on of hands, an intensification of God-awareness. At those times when I was struggling in my Christian life, that touch and laying-on of hands brought a unique experience of God's sanctifying presence into my life. I was never the same after those experiences. We still need altar services like these in our churches!

I am also suggesting to you, friends, that we need a revival of true sanctification among the people of God. In recent years, sanctification has come to be such an ambiguous experience in many churches that you never know when it occurs. According to many people's way of thinking, somewhere between your new birth and your death, sanctification just somehow "happens" within you, through some kind of spiritual osmosis.

I do believe sanctification is a process, not an instantaneous once-and-for-all occurrence. But, friends, within the *process of sanctification* there should be many definable *works of sanctification*. Our people need to be delivered from habits. They need to be healed from past hurts. These are targets for the sanctifying grace of God.

We must help our people find the deliverance and healing they need through the touch of God's presence at our altars. For it's only as they are delivered from those carnal habits and healed of the hurts in their lives that their bodies can function according to their divine purpose, as temples of the Holy Spirit. *Then* they can go as lights into the darkness. As salt to heal the rot in our world. As fire to warm others and draw them to the Father. Hallelujah!

### Into the highways and byways

We will never bring today's world into the church to get saved. We have to get God's people healed and delivered so they can take His presence out where the world is! In the process, we're going to have to teach them how to talk about Jesus to people who don't know Him. We don't know how to talk to people who are divorced. We don't know how to talk to homosexuals. We don't know how to talk to drug addicts. We have *come out* so far from among them and become so *separate* that we're not at home with sinners.

When our bodies become His temples and His Spirit dwells within us, the same Spirit that made Jesus the friend of sinners will make the people of our churches the friends of sinners! And we won't need to worry about them compromising. They'll learn the difference between acceptance and approval. We don't approve of the world's way of living, but we must learn to accept them and love them as people. And we can't do that unless we understand their problems and can talk to them in terms of their needs.

As we hold these emblems in our hands today, may they make us aware of Christ's presence. When we hold them in our hands, may we pray, *O, God, make me utterly dependent on Jesus. Help me to dedicate my body as a temple where Your Spirit dwells. In becoming a friend of sinners, Lord, don't let me be so much like them that they can't see a difference between me and them. Let there be a holy and healthy uniqueness about me.*

Let us teach our people to do good to all people. This is the first step in evangelism. Jesus taught us, *"Let your light so shine before men that they may see your good works, and glorify your Father which is in heaven."*[16] Let's teach people how to have compassion for those who are in prison, for those who are ill, for those who are poor, those who are homeless—and also for those who are rich, but understand the emptiness of their riches.

Let's help our people understand that the devil who tore the physical body of Christ to pieces is very active in trying to tear His Body, the Church, to pieces. Now, he's not trying to destroy the Church because of its size. The devil does not need to fear a big Church. He can manage that without any problem. But he trembles before a *united* Church.

### A united Body of Christ is a powerful force!

When Dolores and I were going through our illnesses a few months ago, we began to understand—as perhaps never before in our lives—the tremendous power within the Body of Christ for healing. When we were at places where we couldn't pray for ourselves, we found God laying us on the hearts of scores of people who were able to pray for us and believe for us. Please don't misunderstand me. It would have been tremendously difficult for me to have learned to live without her and, I suspect, for her to have learned to live without me, but we would not have taken it as a defeat of our faith had the Lord chosen to take either one of us into His presence.

One of the ways the Lord uses Pentecostal people in a unique way is through signs and wonders and gifts of healing. However, whether or not we're healed shouldn't be a test of the validity of our faith or the sanctity of our life. As long as the Body of Christ is sufficiently united for God to manifest himself among us, there will be enough of us supernaturally healed to stop the mouths of every gainsayer in the world. We don't want to discredit excellent medical care. We've had that, and we appreciate it. But beyond what doctors could do, there came from the Body of Christ a healing presence into our home and into our lives because the Body of Christ was *functioning as the Body of Christ.*

I don't know what healing you need in your life today, what habit needs to be broken, or what part of your history the enemy is still using to cripple you. I do know that if we can discern the Lord's Body in what we do today, chains will drop off of this group. Painful sores in our souls will be touched by *"a balm in Gilead."*[17] Hallelujah be to God! If we can discern the Lord's Body in what we do today, many of us will no longer be weak or sickly. Many of us will have added days and weeks and months and years to celebrate the real purpose for which we live: *"so now also [that] Christ shall be magnified in my body, whether it be by life or by death. For to me to live is Christ, and to die is gain."*[18]

### Overturning tables in the temple of the Lord

My body serves its highest purpose when it becomes the Lord's temple. And as Jesus plaited the whip and drove the moneychangers out of the physical temple, may we examine ourselves this morning and see how many tables need to be overturned in our lives. May we see how much dung needs to be swept out of our temple. May we realize how God longs to have our temple solely occupied by His presence.

When we go back to our churches, then, let's help them to discern the Lord's Body when we come together, so that *"the sin which so easily entangles us"* might be dropped and we might all learn to *"run with endurance the race that is set before us, fixing our eyes on Jesus, the author and perfecter of [our] faith, who for the joy set before him endured the cross, despising the shame, and has sat down at the right hand of the throne of God."*[19]

Shall we bow our hearts in prayer.

*Father, as we prepare to bring ourselves to the Lord's Table once again, we pray that You will help us to discern His Body, rightly judge His Body, and realize what a sacrifice of love He made for us. What a demonstration of the power of sin was evidenced in His cruel death. But His magnificent resurrection demonstrated an even greater power than the power of sin that had nailed Him to that cross. That greater power quickened Jesus' body and raised Him from the dead. And that power is here today to quicken us, heal us, and fill us with Christ's presence.*

*Help us to push everything out of our lives that would deprive Jesus of the place He deserves in our lives. May we truly become living sacrifices, holy and acceptable unto God.* [20]

*O, God, we pray for those who may be struggling with habits and secret sins they are frightened to surface. We can be so judgmental. And it's difficult for those who are leaders in the church to know where to turn and what to do when they see in their own temples things that need to be driven out. Let it happen this morning, intimately, personally, privately, while we share these emblems of Your broken body. And may there come among us, Lord, an intensification of our awareness of Your Presence that makes us long to celebrate Communion with our brothers and sisters. Make us determined to submit ourselves to You, to keep Your Body united when the enemy would tear us apart.*

*We offer ourselves to You, Lord. Come and move in our temples and through our lives. Challenge us to take You, Lord, like light into darkness and like salt into corruption. We long to be used for the purpose for which we've been created. And may our time around Your Table today remind us of the tremendous privilege of serving You. In Jesus' Name, Amen.*

The brethren are coming now to serve you the emblems of the Lord's Supper. While you're being served, we'll worship the Lord in song. When everyone is served, we will partake of the emblems together.

"Oh, the blood of Jesus; Oh, the blood of Jesus;
Oh, the blood of Jesus; it washes white as snow."

"At the Cross"
"When I Survey the Wondrous Cross"
"My Jesus, I Love Thee"
"Where He Leads Me, I Will Follow"

Let's bow our hearts before the Lord.

*Holy Spirit, move among us this morning. Help us to examine ourselves so that we eat of the bread discerning and understanding that it represents Your body that was torn because of our sin. Oh, God, we believe that the body of Your Son was torn so that our bodies could be made whole. We believe that He was wounded for our transgressions; bruised for our iniquities; we believe that the chastisement of our peace was upon Him, and that with His stripes we were healed. Lord, we ask that You would move among us. With the eating of this bread, as definitely as through the laying-on of hands and the anointing with oil, let healing and deliverance flow among us. Wherever the need may be, meet it, Lord. May we look back upon this time and this place as the moment and place where God broke through and touched us because, in eating the bread, we judged Your Body rightly. In Jesus' Name we pray, Amen.*

Shall we eat the bread together.

*And as we hold the cup this morning, Father, remind us how repugnant it was for Jesus to take on himself the sins of the world. Only His love for You and His love for us could compel Him to do it. Lord, help us to understand the deceitful nature of our own hearts. Help us never to be converted to the myth that Christians don't sin. For, if we say that we have no sin, we only deceive ourselves. You are not deceived.*

*Help us to teach our people what to do when we sin. Oh, God, make repentance and confession commonplace among us. Make it easy for the people of God to be honest about their sins in the house of God.*

*We ask you to help us be honest about our sins. I ask you to help me to be honest about my sins. And as I drink this cup, Lord, may I not be like a Pharisee and feel that I'm not like the rest of those who are here today. Oh, God, help me to know—help us all to know—that the only difference between us and those who are living in disobedience is the grace of God. Our salvation is by grace through faith, and not of works, lest anyone should boast.*

*And help us this morning to be privately but openly honest with You about our sins. And as we confess our sins, remind us that you're faithful and just to forgive us our sins and to cleanse us from all unrighteousness. As we drink this cup, may we discern that the blood of Jesus Christ, Your Son, cleanses us from every sin we're honest enough to confess to You. And when we're honest enough to confess, You even forgive us of the sins of which we know nothing, for You have promised through Christ not only to forgive us of our sins but to cleanse us from all unrighteousness. We thank You for that cleansing as we celebrate it together through the drinking of the cup. In Jesus' Name, Amen.*

Shall we take the cup together.

Let's praise God together as we sing: "To God Be the Glory."

---

[1] 1 Corinthians 11:17-33, NASB.

[2] Isaiah 14:12-15.

[3] Genesis 2:7.

[4] Genesis 3:1-24.

[5] Genesis 1:28.

[6] Colossians 2:9.

[7] 1 Timothy 3:16.

[8] John 15:13.

[9] Romans 5:8.

[10] John 10:17,18.

[11] 1 Corinthians 11:24.

[12] Luke 22:20.

[13] 2 Corinthians 4:4.

[14] 1 Corinthians 6:19,20.

[15] A reference to Paul's explanation to the Athenians on Mars' Hill of the nature of the Christian God and each believer's relationship to God through Christ; Acts 17:28. He had just told them that God doesn't dwell in man-made temples or in the "things" given to Him, but in the lives of His followers–just as they "live, and move, and have [their] being" in Him.

[16] Matthew 5:16..

[17] Jeremiah 46:11.

[18] Philippians 1:20,21.

[19] Hebrews 12:1,2, NASB

[20] Romans 12:1.

# 7

## Recognizing the Body of the Lord *

*We sit here in this service today, Father, a living manifestation of the miraculous power of the Lord Jesus Christ to gather together in one body people who in the natural would never have met in this world. We don't understand the mystery of your grace that through the preaching of the gospel and the exaltation of Jesus Christ, You draw us, who are so different, into one body so that we may become laborers together with You in reconciling to You this world for whom Christ died.*

*This morning, lift us above our own individual spheres of responsibility. Help us to lay aside those ambitions that at times can be so narrowly defined and selfish, even though they are focused upon our zeal for a particular part of Your work. Help us see the One who brings us together. Help us see ourselves as members of His Body, of His flesh, and of His bones.*[1] *May we allow His mind to orchestrate our efforts, His heart to vitalize our efforts, and His will to sustain our efforts until the whole world knows Jesus. These things we pray in His name and for His glory, Amen.*

Twice in Paul's first letter to the Corinthian church, he speaks of the Lord's Supper. Perhaps the best way we can put these passages into focus would be to simply read them, starting with 1 Corinthians 10:1-22 (NIV). This is a passage seldom read during Communion services; and yet, the obvious reference is there as we read:

> *"For I do not want you to be ignorant of the fact, brothers, that our forefathers were all under the cloud and that*

---

* Sermon for the Communion Service of the 1991 Ohio District Council of the Assemblies of God, Bethel Temple, Parma, Ohio.

*they all passed through the sea. They were all baptized into Moses in the cloud and in the sea. They all ate the same spiritual food and drank the same spiritual drink; for they drank from the spiritual rock that accompanied them, and that rock was Christ. Nevertheless, God was not pleased with most of them; their bodies were scattered over the desert.*

"*Now these things occurred as examples to keep us from setting our hearts on evil things as they did. Do not be idolaters, as some of them were; as it is written: 'The people sat down to eat and drink and got up to indulge in pagan revelry.' We should not commit sexual immorality, as some of them did—and in one day twenty-three thousand of them died. We should not test the Lord, as some of them did—and were killed by snakes. And do not grumble, as some of them did—and were killed by the destroying angel.*

"*These things happened to them as examples and were written down as warnings for us, on whom the fulfillment of the ages has come. So, if you think you are standing firm, be careful that you don't fall! No temptation has seized you except what is common to man. And God is faithful; he will not let you be tempted beyond what you can bear. But when you are tempted, he will also provide a way out so that you can stand up under it.*

"*Therefore, my dear friends, flee from idolatry. I speak to sensible people; judge for yourselves what I say. Is not the cup of thanksgiving for which we give thanks a participation in the blood of Christ? And is not the bread that we break a participation in the body of Christ? Because there is one loaf, we, who are many, are one body, for we all partake of the one loaf.*

"*Consider the people of Israel: Do not those who eat the sacrifices participate in the altar? Do I mean then that a sacrifice offered to an idol is anything, or that an idol is anything? No, but the sacrifices of pagans are offered to demons, not to God, and I do not want you to be participants with demons. You cannot drink the cup of the Lord and the cup of demons too; you cannot have a part in both the Lord's table and the table of demons. Are we trying to arouse the Lord's jealousy? Are we stronger than he?*

In this tenth chapter of 1 Corinthians, Paul points out the contradiction of Christians sitting at the Lord's Table and also at the table of the gods of this world. He says this is largely because they fail to see the contradictions in their lives—fail to recognize the Body of the Lord. We who are members of His Body attempt to make ourselves members of this world as well.

Now let's look at 1 Corinthians 11:17-33 (NIV):

*"In the following directives I have no praise for you, for your meetings do more harm than good. In the first place, I hear that when you come together as a church, there are divisions among you, and to some extent I believe it. No doubt there have to be differences among you to show which of you have God's approval. When you come together, it is not the Lord's Supper you eat, for as you eat, each of you goes ahead without waiting for anybody else. One remains hungry, another gets drunk. Don't you have homes to eat and drink in? Or do you despise the church of God and humiliate those who have nothing? What shall I say to you? Shall I praise you for this? Certainly not!*

*"For I received from the Lord what I also passed on to you: The Lord Jesus, on the night he was betrayed, took bread, and when he had given thanks, he broke it and said, 'This is my body, which is broken for you; do this in remembrance of me.' In the same way, after supper he took the cup, saying, 'This cup is the new covenant in my blood; do this, whenever you drink it, in remembrance of me.' For whenever you eat this bread and drink this cup, you proclaim the Lord's death until he comes.*

*"Therefore, whoever eats the bread or drinks the cup of the Lord in an unworthy manner will be guilty of sinning against the body and blood of the Lord. A man ought to examine himself before he eats of the bread and drinks of the cup. For anyone who eats and drinks without recognizing the body of the Lord eats and drinks judgment on himself. That is why many among you are weak and sick, and a number of you have fallen asleep. But if we judged ourselves, we would not come under judgment.*

*When we are judged by the Lord, we are being disciplined so that we will not be condemned with the world.*

*"So then, my brothers, when you come together to eat, wait for each other. If anyone is hungry, he should eat at home, so that when you meet together it may not result in judgment."*

Let's turn now to 1 Corinthians 12:12-27 (NIV):

*"The body is a unit, though it is made up of many parts; and though all its parts are many, they form one body. So it is with Christ. For we were all baptized by one Spirit into one body—whether Jews or Greeks, slave or free—and we were all given the one Spirit to drink.*

*"Now the body is not made up of one part, but of many. If the foot should say, 'Because I am not a hand, I do not belong to the body,' it would not for that reason cease to be part of the body. And if the ear should say, 'Because I am not an eye, I do not belong to the body,' it would not for that reason cease to be part of the body. If the whole body were an eye, where would the sense of hearing be? If the whole body were an ear, where would the sense of smell be? But in fact God has arranged the parts in the body, every one of them, just as He wanted them to be. If they were all one part, where would the body be? As it is, there are many parts, but one body.*

*"The eye cannot say to the hand, 'I don't need you!' And the head cannot say to the feet, 'I don't need you!' On the contrary, those parts of the body that seem to be weaker are indispensable, and the parts that we think are less honorable we treat with special honor. And the parts that are unpresentable are treated with special modesty, while our presentable parts need no special treatment. But God has combined the members of the body and has given greater honor to the parts that lacked it, so that there should be no division in the body, but that its parts should have equal concern for each other. If one part suffers, every part suffers with it; if one part is honored, every part rejoices with it.*

*"Now you are the body of Christ, and each one of you is a part of it."*

Now let's go to the more traditional Communion passage, which is 1 Corinthians 11:23-31 (NIV). This was also included in the more lengthy passage already quoted from that chapter:

" . . . *The Lord Jesus, on the night he was betrayed, took bread, and when he had given thanks, he broke it and said, 'This is my body, which is for you; do this in remembrance of me.'*

*"In the same way, after supper he took the cup, saying, 'This cup is the new covenant in my blood; do this, whenever you drink it, in remembrance of me.' For whenever you eat this bread and drink this cup, you proclaim the Lord's death until he comes.*

*"Therefore, whoever eats the bread or drinks the cup of the Lord in an unworthy manner will be guilty of sinning against the body and blood of the Lord. A man ought to examine himself before he eats of the bread and drinks of the cup. For anyone who eats and drinks without recognizing the body of the Lord eats and drinks judgment on himself. That is why many among you are weak and sick, and a number of you have fallen asleep. But if we judged ourselves, we would not come under judgment."*

Our focus is on verse 29: *"Anyone who eats and drinks without recognizing the body of the Lord eats and drinks judgment on himself."*

The Eucharist, or Communion, was historically celebrated at the end of a shared meal known as the Lord's Supper. Paul insisted that there was nothing magical or superstitious about the Eucharist. He would be the first, loudest, and most effective antagonist against the doctrine of transubstantiation. The extent to which believers were blessed by partaking of Communion was determined by their willingness to examine themselves and recognize the Lord's body and blood as being symbolically reflected in the bread and the cup. I would like for us to focus on recognizing the body and blood of the Lord in three ways.

### Recognizing the Lord's historic body and blood

When we take the bread and the cup, we understand that they represent the historical, physical body of Jesus. In that body, He was literally wounded for our transgressions and bruised for our iniquities. He literally took upon himself our chastisement, and our healing was purchased with His stripes.[2] So when we recognize the Lord's physical body in the elements, we are saying Jesus is a real person. We recognize the historical Jesus. We believe that He was delivered up to a cruel and painful death for our offenses. We believe that He was raised again for our justification. That's the *historical dimension* of recognizing the Lord's body.

### The future Body of Christ

The Lord's body also has a future meaning for us. Jesus said, when He instituted the Eucharist with His disciples, *"I will not drink henceforth of this fruit of the vine, until that day when I drink it new with you in my Father's kingdom."*[3] So, as we take the emblems this morning, we need to recognize the Body and blood of the Lord in a historic sense, in a future or prophetic sense, and in an ongoing or present sense.

### The present Body of Christ

As we take the bread and the cup this morning, we need to recognize that the Church as the Lord's present Body on earth is distinct from pagans. We are not speaking now of His physical, historic, resurrected body. We are speaking of the Church as the representative Body of the Lord here on earth at this moment.

These elements not only represent what Christ *did* for us but they also represent what Christ *is now doing* for us. He is very active on our behalf this morning. He *"ever liveth to make intercession"* for us at God's right hand.[4] I appreciated our district superintendent's message about that last night, about how real the temptations of Jesus were; how *He experienced* our weaknesses, our faults, our failures, our shortcomings, and our weariness of heart. And today as we observe Communion in our weaknesses, in our faults, in our failures, in our shortcomings, in our weariness—these elements remind us that Jesus is alive and at the right hand of the Father, interceding on our behalf. He is with us just as He was with Peter in faltering moments of the apostle's life. He reminded Peter, *"Satan hath desired to have you, that he may sift you as wheat, but I have prayed for thee."*[5] And, He is praying for you and me today.

No doubt some of you are very discouraged—while others are at the peak of victory. The Lord needs to humble some of us and exalt others. In His wisdom, He wants to bring some of us down and lift others of us up. This is part of His *present ministry* on our behalf at the right hand of the Father. We need to recognize His bodily presence at the right hand of the Father, *right now, today, forever living to make intercession for us* as we take the bread and the cup.

When we think of pagans, we think of ancient civilizations' mythical gods or other more recent tribal nations with their totem poles and war paint. However, I want you to think of the primary symbols of *American paganism*: our checkbooks. If you want to know how often the Body of Christ sits at the table of the gods of this world, consider what social researchers are saying about the way we Americans spend our money.

First, there is no significant difference between the checkbook entries of the average churchgoer and those of the unbeliever in the United States. We don't have witch doctors with feather headdresses or war chants accompanied by primitive drums in our society. However, that isn't to say we don't have either of these elements.

The advertising executives of Madison Avenue are our witch doctors; they cast the magic spells on us. And our tribal dances come with predictable frequency: six or seven times per hour on our electronic "jungle drum," which we call a television. Our witch doctors create in our children and adults alike a desire to be like the people they see warding off 20th century evil spirits with all manner of consumer goods—they learn to want what the witch-doctor sponsors are selling.

### You can only serve one God at a time

Paul begins the tenth chapter of 1 Corinthians by using the analogy of God's dealings with Israel to teach these fairly new Greek Christians the dangers of compromising their Christian identity. In verse 11, he clearly states that what happened to Israel was meant to be an example of what happens when God's people betray their identity.

In the Old Testament, we read how Israel had the Passover Lamb, protection from devastating plagues, a baptism in the sea, manna from heaven, a cloud of smoke by day, and a heavenly pillar of fire by night to identify them as God's chosen people. However, none of these things could protect them from the appeal of sitting at the tables of pagan gods worshipped by the Canaanite peoples they were sent to conquer.

*Falling in love with the pagan gods of this world* was Israel's greatest sin. Even though they still kept the Passover, *they so compromised their identity by becoming familiar with the gods of this world* that soon it was hard to see any difference between the Israelites and the people who surrounded them. Only on their Hebrew feast days was there much difference between the Israelites and the pagans.

**You can only serve one god at a time . . . who will it be?**

In much the same way, the Corinthians were attending the feasts of pagans while mistakenly believing that the Eucharist gave them miraculous protection from any intrusion of demon spirits. Paul was trying to help them get their spiritual eyes open to the danger inherent in such activities. *"You cannot serve God and mammon;"*[6] you cannot serve the One True God and Satan at the same time. One reason this is true is that the god you serve exerts a tremendous influence on your mind; on your thoughts and behaviors. You radiate the presence of that god in the things you do and say, and in the way you conduct your life. There is only room for one god at a time in your life.

*The god of this world* controls the minds of *people who are "of" this world.* (That is why believers are to be *"in"* the world but not *"of"* the world[7]—we are to be different because we are not "of" the god of this world.) Jesus reminded the Father that, *"I have manifested thy name unto the men which thou gavest me out of the world: thine they were, and thou gavest them me; and they have kept thy word."*[8] We are God's people; not Satan's.

Governments largely controlled by the god of this world define and operate the institutions of this world. Those institutions include courts, schools, old-age pensions, military might and deployment, federal budgets, agriculture, commerce, public utilities, medical care . . . the list is endless.

American "institutions," with the exception of the "institutional church," correspond to the 14 positions in every president's cabinet of advisers. Those advisers are the Secretaries of State . . . Treasury . . . Defense . . . the Interior . . . Agriculture . . . Commerce . . . Labor . . .

Health and Human Services . . . Housing and Urban Development . . . Transportation . . . Energy . . . Education . . . Veterans Affairs . . . our Surgeon General and our Attorney General. The life of every American citizen is impacted by the decisions these cabinet members reach.

When initial decisions are made by a godless government, and later revisions are made in the same way by successive leaders, it stands to reason that the older a nation becomes the more ungodly its institutions become and the greater the manifestation of evil in that society.

I believe our nation is on a very dangerous course. And while I do not believe that it is too late for our country to turn back to God, I must confess I don't see signs of that happening. And before it *can* happen, the Christians of this nation first need to understand what it means to be the Body of the Lord, and then we need to declare our position.

We are a people who have been called out from the pagan world around us to demonstrate the uniqueness of our divine origin. If we fail to demonstrate this, we are failing God in His desire to bring our country back to God.

Paul admonished the Corinthians, *don't trust in your observance of the Eucharist for protection from the god of this world; it's not going to happen. Rather, flee idolatry! You cannot partake of the table of pagans and still belong at the Table of the Lord.* Remember what Jesus said in the Sermon on the Mount, and we've already referred to it once: *"You cannot serve God and mammon."* And mammon, or money, is the god of pagans. Do you know how the dictionary defines mammon? It is, "material wealth or possessions, especially [those] having a debasing influence."

### A chosen generation

When we properly discern the present Body of the Lord, we recognize that we are a people who have been called out from the pagan world around us to be unique; to be representatives of God's light in a dark world. *"But ye are a chosen generation, a royal priesthood, an holy nation, a peculiar people; that ye should shew forth the praises of him who hath called you out of darkness into his marvellous light . . . which . . . are now the people of God."*[9]

How are we to demonstrate that we sit at a different table; that we identify with the One True God? By the fruit of His Spirit in our lives. By our works. *"Let your light so shine before men, that they may see your good works, and glorify your Father which is in heaven."*[10] How do we do that? *"As we therefore have opportunity, let us do good unto all men, especially unto them who are of the household of faith."*[11] That is how we recognize and participate in the Lord's Body at this present time on earth.

### Divine energy for a God-given task

We are strengthened for the task *"... with all might, according to his glorious power."*[12] Paul is talking about those moments in each person's life when we recognize the Lord's Body as Thomas did, and the truth bursts in on us that we are in the presence of Jesus. At that moment there comes to us an energy that is not of flesh and blood!

A legalistic response to a call to prayer will weary your flesh. You will feel like *they that wait upon the Lord waste their time.* You'll be thinking about all the things you ought to be doing and planning and organizing and administering and . . . the list goes on and on. There is also *a bureaucratic energy* that comes along with institutional Christianity. At times, we don't recognize the difference between divine and institutional energy. But the prophet knew the difference: *"They that wait upon the Lord shall renew their strength; they shall mount up with wings as eagles; they shall run, and not be weary; and they shall walk, and not faint."*[13] You don't get that kind of energy when you sit at the table of this world.

Last night, as our district superintendent was leading us in our opening rally, I became aware of intense energy in our midst—from the corporate Body of Christ. Do you know what that kind of energy is for? Among other things, it's to strengthen the Body!

We are called to a lifestyle that is as different from the lifestyle of this world as light is from darkness. And when that difference is no longer there, *"if the salt have lost his savour . . . it is thenceforth good for nothing, but to be cast out, and to be trodden under foot of men."*[14]

And so, this morning, let us recognize the Lord's body as separating us from the world. As we eat and drink together this morning, may we determine to *be different.* We are called to give the world a contrast; to shine as the stars of the firmament in a sin-darkened world.

## The inclusiveness of the Lord's Body

His present Body is not only to be separate from the world; the parts of His Body are to be united and joined together with each other. There was a time, a decade or so ago, when one of my great anxieties for the Church was that we would buy the *homogeneous* principle of church growth. I was afraid we would end up with a form of Christianity for the rich and a form of Christianity for the poor; a form of Christianity for those with graduate degrees and a form of Christianity for those who didn't even go to high school.

That's what was going on in Corinth. The few free and lettered men in the church were giving voice to a temptation we all face at various times in our growth and development. They were talking about knowing one's station in life, and staying in it: *". . . ye see your calling, brethren. . . ."*[15] In 20th century church jargon, this would translate as, "Well, you know, our church is becoming recognized in the community." "We have a number of medical doctors who come to our church." "Several university professors attend our church."

## Class consciousness has no place in the Body of Christ

What does it matter that doctors or professors or attorneys attend your church? What are you trying to tell me? You haven't mentioned the factory workers or garbage collectors who come to your church . . . you haven't told me about the struggling single mom who scrubs supermarket floors at night . . . are you hearing what I'm saying?

This is the *Corinthian spirit.* The free people. The business people. In Corinth, they didn't want to sit or share their meal with slaves who were probably uncouth and might not have had a bath lately. It was relatively easy for those of the upper level of Corinthian society to avoid the less fortunate citizens—even in the church. The slaves didn't control their own time. They were not free men, so they could only come when their day's work was done. The free men could eat any time, so they collaborated and got together at a different time from the poorer believers. Paul says, *"This [attitude] is why many are weak and sickly among you."*[16]

In this eleventh chapter of 1 Corinthians, he focused not only on the *contradiction* of a divided church eating from a common loaf and drinking from a common cup; he also addressed the *reason* for such a division. The wealthier, socially elite members of the congregation were holding themselves apart from those members who were of lower social rank. We'll come back to this thought in a moment.

Many of us grew up during a very legalistic time in Pentecost—when partaking of Communion was comparable to subjecting oneself to the "jealousy test" of the Old Testament. This was when a man who was suspicious that his wife had committed adultery would bring her to the door of the tabernacle to be tested by the priest. He would mix a concoction of water and dust from the holy place and force her to drink it. If she was guilty as accused, then she would rot from her thigh, her belly would swell up, and she would die. But if she was innocent, she would conceive and bear a son.

People took Communion like that, totally blind to the spiritual "elitism" that was behind that kind of spiritual *superiority complex* because they didn't *rot and die.* We brandished our holiness in gravy-spotted black ties in those days . . . totally unaware that the very elitism that Paul was referring to *socially* had crept into our *spirit.*

What Paul is saying here is that *this kind of observance of the Lord's Supper* is a mockery to God. If you can't wait for one another, so that the poor and the rich eat together, the unlettered and the lettered eat together, then do away with the preceding meal and just focus on the bread and the cup.

### The Body of Christ lives on both sides of the tracks

We're finally beginning to recognize that some of Christ's Body is in the ghetto areas of our cities. Some of the Body lives on the wrong side of the tracks. For a long time, we've recognized that parts of the Body of Christ live in Africa and Asia and the Hispanic nations. We've been perfectly willing to send people to minister among the disadvantaged ethnic communities of our nation . . . but we haven't wanted to mix and mingle with those people *in the same church.*

My friend, the devil does not care how big the Church becomes. He does not fear a *big* Church. He fears a *united* Church. And he was afraid of that in the local Corinthian church. I can almost hear him saying to them, *Go ahead and eat with the other rich men and scholars. Don't wait for the less fortunate among you; don't think about what it means to recognize the Body and Blood in those emblems. Just eat and drink and go your merry way. You've got things to do.* How is that any different from what we do today? Christ often finds us celebrating Communion at the end of a busy Sunday morning service, just before the rush toward the fast food places. In this kind of hurried environment, very few among us take time to recognize Christ's Body and blood in those emblems.

### The bread and the cup are powerful reminders of the Body and blood of Christ, but they are not magical

Remember, there is nothing magical in the bread and the cup that will protect us from the ravages of the god of this world. There's nothing magical in these emblems that will make us live one bit different next week from the way we lived last week, until we recognize that these emblems are a reminder that we are to be different from the world, a unique people unto God. Your life and mine should look different not only to those who view it from afar, but also to those who live with us in the same home. Our protection and empowerment come in recognizing the Body and blood of the Lord in the emblems of Communion.

There's nothing about these emblems that will automatically make us all enjoy the same style of worship. Some of us shout it . . . others of us sing it . . . some with the volume turned clear up and some in a much quieter fashion . . . some of us sing from the hymnals and some from *off the wall* with overhead projectors and chorus sheets. Some of us raise our hands in a posture of surrender and others in a posture of taking or receiving.

Each of us must recognize that sincere worship may occur in any of these forms that appeal to our various brothers and sisters in the Lord; other members of the same Body of which we're a part. And that's okay. We are still "one in the bonds of love." *We will make hell tremble* only when we genuinely recognize the Lord's Body and become one under the lordship of Christ.

We're going to conclude this morning with these words from our Lord's high priestly prayer:

*"I have given them thy word; and the world hath hated them, because they are not of the world, even as I am not of the world. I pray not that thou shouldest take them out of the world, but that thou shouldest keep them from the evil. They are not of the world, even as I am not of the world. Sanctify them through thy truth: thy word is truth.*

*"As thou hast sent me into the world, even so have I also sent them into the world. And for their sakes I sanctify myself, that they also might be sanctified through the truth. Neither pray I for these alone, but for them also which shall believe on me through their word; That they all may be one; as thou, Father, art in me, and I in thee, that they also may be one in us: that the world may believe that thou hast sent me.*

*"And the glory which thou gavest me I have given them; that they may be one, even as we are one: I in them, and thou in me, that they may be made perfect in one; and that the world may know that thou hast sent me, and hast loved them, as thou hast loved me.*

*"Father, I will that they also, whom thou hast given me, be with me where I am; that they may behold my glory, which thou hast given me: for thou lovedst me before the foundation of the world."*[17]

Shall we pray as we prepare for the Lord's Supper.

*Today, Father, let each of us feel the unity of the family that can only come when Your Spirit in each of our hearts enables us to call you Our Father. Our birth into Your family came at so great a price. And Lord Jesus, as we take the bread and the cup today and pause to remember those who are now with You—as You long for all of us to be—remind us that these elements are not common things. They are Your gift to us, to remind us of Your physical body that was broken and Your blood that was shed; of Your hands that would soon become nail-scarred on our behalf.*

*Remind us that we take these emblems in tribute to Your eternal intercession on our behalf; in anticipation of Your soon return to earth crowned with the glory that belongs to You alone.*

*Help us to see that every time we compromise our Christian life, we cheapen the sacrifice Christ made on Calvary to make us different from the pagans of this world. And make us willing to extend ourselves to our brothers . . . to our sisters . . . until we desire, like Paul, to be " .* . . made all things to all men, that [we] might by all means save some."[18] *In Jesus' Name, we pray, Amen.*

---

[1] Ephesians 5:30.
[2] Isaiah 53:5.
[3] Matthew 26:29.
[4] Hebrews 7:25.
[5] Luke 22:31,32.
[6] Matthew 6:24.
[7] John 17:11-16.
[8] John 17:6.
[9] 1 Peter 2:9,10.
[10] Matthew 5:16.
[11] Galatians 6:10.
[12] Colossians 1:11.
[13] Isaiah 40:31.
[14] Matthew 5:13.
[15] 1 Corinthians 1:26.
[16] 1 Corinthians 11:30.
[17] John 17:14-24.
[18] 1 Corinthians 9:22.

# 8

# Self-Examination at the
# Table of the Lord *

I'm aware that I've been standing in the strength of other people's prayers. The night before last, Dolores asked me to pray that Jesus would just take her in His arms. She was that ready to go be with Him. I have mixed feelings about that, but *I know I can never love her like Jesus loves her. And He can care for her now; I can't.* Her body is dissolving . . . but her spirit is stronger than ever. The hospice team is with her today . . . our children have been fantastic to help care for her . . . and *I'm here today at her command* . . . not just with her permission. She wanted me to be here and I'm happy both to convey her love to each of you and to take your love back to her.[1]

The Lord knew I needed some reassurance about this morning's message. Both manifestations of His presence we've just had here confirm the direction in which He has led me to prepare my comments. I believe this is something He wants us to hear before we come to His Table today. We're going to start with a rather long passage of Scripture:

> *"But in giving this instruction, I do not praise you,*
> *because you come together not for the better but for the worse.*
> *For, in the first place, when you come together as a church, I*
> *hear that divisions exist among you; and in part, I believe it.*
> *For there must also be factions among you, in order that those*
> *who are approved may have become evident among you.*

---

* Sermon for the Communion Service of the 1992 Ohio District Council of the Assemblies of God, Calvary Assembly of God, Toledo, Ohio.

*Therefore when you meet together, it is not to eat the Lord's Supper, for in your eating, each one takes his own supper first; and one is hungry, and another is drunk. What! Do you not have houses in which to eat and drink? Or do you despise the church of God, and shame those who have nothing? What shall I say to you? Shall I praise you? In this, I will not praise you.*

*"For I received from the Lord that which also I delivered to you, that the Lord Jesus in the night in which He was betrayed took bread; and when He had given thanks, He broke it, and said, 'This is my body, which is for you; do this in remembrance of Me.'*

*"In the same way He took the cup also, after supper, saying, 'This cup is the new covenant in My blood; do this, as often as you drink it, in remembrance of Me.' For as often as you eat this bread and drink the cup, you proclaim the Lord's death until He comes.*

*"Therefore, whoever eats the bread or drinks the cup of the Lord in an unworthy manner, shall be guilty of the body and the blood of the Lord. But let a man examine himself, and so let him eat of the bread and drink of the cup. For he who eats and drinks, eats and drinks judgment to himself, if he does not judge the body rightly. For this reason, many among you are weak and sick, and a number sleep. But if we judged ourselves rightly, we should not be judged. But when we are judged, we are disciplined by the Lord in order that we may not be condemned along with the world.*

*"So then, my brethren, when you come together to eat, wait for one another. If anyone is hungry, let him eat at home, so that you may not come together for judgment."*[2]

Shall we bow our hearts in prayer.

*Father, we tend to grow up so conscious of what others think of us, and so careful about our appearance before other people, but we think so little about how our inner person appears to You when we meet You face to face at the Table of the Lord. Help us to care more for how our inner person appears before You than for how our outer person appears before others. It is before You, not others, that we stand or fall, because it is before You that each of us must give an account of our own self as we enter into eternity.*

*This is one of the reasons why, in mercy, You bring us to Your Table regularly, pleading with us to be open and honest and transparent in our self-examination. You want to help us walk before You worthy of the vocation whereunto we have been called, as your representatives here on earth. And in that day, when we stand before You, we truly want to hear these words:* "Well done, thou good and faithful servant."[3] *In Jesus' name we pray, Amen.*

Paul begins 1 Corinthians, chapter 11, by praising the Corinthians for holding firmly to certain traditions. However, as he begins to discuss their celebration of the Lord's Supper and Communion—for these are two separate events—he changes to a different tone of voice. Let's look at portions of the Scripture reading again with this in mind.

### The Corinthian church was a divided church

In verse 17, Paul says: *"But in giving this instruction, I do not praise you, because you come together not for the better but for the worse."* Notice the confrontation. Paul did not want to believe that the Corinthian church was so divided. But the reports he had received left him no choice: *"For in the first place, when you come together as a church,"* he writes, *"I hear that divisions exist among you. And in part, I believe it."*

Paul was particularly grieved by the magnitude of these divisions, because the Lord's Supper and Communion were celebrations intended to express unity in the Church. Earlier in this same letter, he had written, *"Is not the cup of blessing which we bless a sharing in the blood of Christ? Is not the bread which we break a sharing in the body of Christ? Since there is one bread, we who are many are one body; for we all partake of the one bread."*[4] The Corinthian Christians were so deeply divided that they would not even unite for the Lord's Supper and Communion. Each group ate apart, by themselves.

### Social class divisions in the Corinthian church

Not only was Paul grieved by the depth of the divisions in the Corinthian church; he was even more deeply grieved by the *nature* of the divisions. For it's obvious as we read this passage of Scripture that the divisions fell largely along socioeconomic lines. How often I have read that phrase—*Do you not have houses?*—never really understanding what Paul was doing with those words. He was addressing those who were well off among the Corinthian believers, for most of the Corinthian people didn't own a house. Only those who were wealthy—the free men—owned property. I don't know how many people in the church at Corinth were either slaves or bond servants. Two or three centuries earlier, however, the ratio of two slaves for every freeborn citizen in the big city-states of Greece was not unusual. In Paul's day, this would still have been quite common.

The rich brought plenty of food and wine to the Lord's Supper, but would not share their bounty with others. That meant that some at the Table were there hungry and without resources . . . while others were stuffed full and even drunk on the excess they had brought: *"For in your eating, each one takes his own supper first; and one is hungry and another is drunk."* This meant, as Paul pointed out in verse 20, that the Corinthian believers were not coming together primarily to eat the Lord's Supper: *" . . . Therefore, when you meet together, it is not to eat the Lord's Supper . . .."* They were coming together, instead, to identify and maintain their factions.

Many Bible commentaries place the more affluent Corinthian Christians in the camp of Apollos—those who preferred receiving the gospel from a silver platter and having it presented by a more elegant orator. The other two leaders in the church who had large, separate followings were apparently Cephas and Paul.[5] The New Testament doesn't say that any of these leaders had *encouraged* the people to behave this way—but it had happened. And this factious spirit of disunity had turned the Lord's Supper and Communion into a time of judgment and chastisement for many Corinthian Christians.

### The church should be free of class lines

This is a little bit off our subject, but just let me say here how pleased I am that, as a district and as a denomination, we are turning our attention to the cities. For, at present, we largely represent an affluent, middle-class, white, suburban faction of the Church. Those who are less well off are not adequately represented among us in the majority of our congregations—but they are God's people, too. They need to be among us and we need to be with them. We will only feel that we are one body—and particularly His body—when more of those who are not so well off find us openly welcoming them into our part of the Body of Christ.

Well, in Corinth, these more affluent believers were eating the bread and drinking the cup of the Lord in an unworthy manner. Let's look again at 1 Corinthians 11: 27,29,32, and 34:

> *"Therefore whoever eats the bread or drinks the cup of the Lord in an unworthy manner, shall be guilty of the body and the blood of the Lord . . . For he who eats and drinks, eats and drinks judgment to himself, if he does not judge the body rightly . . . But when we are judged, we are disciplined by the Lord in order that we may not be condemned along with the world . . . If anyone is hungry, let him eat at home so that you may not come together for judgment."*

### Turning a time of judgment into a time of celebration

After Paul confronts the Corinthian church, he focuses on self-examination. Verses 28 and 31 give the congregation his prescription: *"But let a man examine himself, and so let him eat of the bread and drink of the cup . . . if we judged ourselves rightly, we should not be judged."* Paul had already presented self-examination as a way of gaining God's approval and escaping God's judgment much earlier in this first letter to the Corinthians. He had even used himself as an example:

> *"Do you not know that those who run in a race all run, but only one receives the prize? Run in such a way that you may win. And everyone who competes in the games exercises self-control in all things. They then do it to receive a perishable wreath, but we an imperishable. Therefore I run in such a way, as not without aim; I box in such a way, as not beating the air; but I buffet my body and make it my slave, lest possibly, after I have preached to others, I myself should be disqualified."*[6]

How are we to avoid that embarrassment, that Kingdom humiliation? By self-examination. Paul begins by saying this is the way he runs the race; this is the way he fights the good fight; so that he may not end up disapproved and under judgment. Then he uses Israel as an example to the Corinthians, who thought the observance of baptism and Communion gave them some kind of magical protection so that they didn't need to even *participate* in the race, let alone *run to win*. (There are still people in the church with that kind of belief system. As long as they have been baptized and are regularly receiving Communion, they believe God holds some kind of holy, protective umbrella over them.)

Paul also reminds the Corinthians of all the things they have in common with Israel in this regard. He acknowledges that they may be baptized, and they may come regularly to the Lord's Table. But without self-examination, he adds, their participation in these sacraments only intensifies the judgment they will experience and brings disapproval. Do you remember what it was that kept most of Israel from pleasing God? It was a lack of self-examination.

Not all Christians—even in Corinth—met with disapproval and judgment at the Lord's Table. Paul indicates in 1 Corinthians 11:19 that some of them had already learned the lesson of self-examination and were experiencing God's blessing rather than His judgment on their lives: *"For there must also be factions among you, in order that those who are approved may have become evident among you."*

This sounds harsh, but think about it for a moment. If nobody were disapproved, how would we know who the approved were? If there were no divine judgment dispensed, how would we recognize those who were truly being blessed? And what makes the difference? Self examination: *"But let a man examine himself, and so let him eat of the bread and drink of the cup. For he who eats and drinks, eats and drinks judgment to himself, if he does not judge [discern] the body rightly."*[7]

If Communion is to bring the blessing God intends, we must properly judge or discern the Lord's Body as we approach His Table. What does it mean, to *"discern"* the Lord's Body? How do we *"judge"* the Lord's Body properly? What direction must our self-examination take to bring us among the *"approved"* who are *"blessed"* at the Lord's Table?

### Judging the Lord's physical body

First of all, we must rightly judge the Lord's physical body and blood to be represented by the bread and the cup. The risk we take as ministers is that in handling *holy things*, we lose our reverence for what they represent and allow them to become *common things*. We need to be careful not to do that.

Then, let me tell you three things that I continually bring to the Lord's table and urge you to do the same. I'll preface this disclosure by telling you these are the three things that I fear most for our fellowship. First, I fear the institutionalization of the Assemblies of God. This is what happens when perpetuating the organization becomes more important than perpetuating the mission God has given us to share the whole gospel with the whole world.

Second, I fear the professionalization of the Assemblies of God minister. Don't misunderstand me—I am highly in favor of education and training. Without it, we are like the story told of Don Quixote, who "jumped on his horse and rode off in all directions." We need sound Bible training. We need to know the formulas for sermon arrangement. We need business and finance skills. We need supervisory skill for working with our staff members—both paid and volunteer.

*But the ministry is far more than simply a profession you can learn.* Many years ago I saw a teaser below the headline for a magazine article about the ministry which said, "It is in the terrible, terrible *doing* of the ministry that the minister is *born.*" I have never forgotten that line, nor have I forgotten my response to it. I personally believe that the minister is *born* by a God-given calling. He or she must then have adequate training. The *refining* and *proving* are the things that occur in that awesome and terrifying *doing of the ministry*, as we learn how to love those who seem unlovable and go that second mile. We dare not professionalize the ministry God has given us by trying to make it like any other profession, for which one needs only a good academic background and perhaps a license. The ministry is a God-given calling on one's life.

Third, I fear the intellectualization of the Pentecostal experience—that we will analyze and rationalize and scientifically explain it until we lose our ability to experience and feel this fire from heaven. A person either believes or doesn't believe that this is a very unique way God edifies us both as individual believers and as groups of believers—at various times and for various reasons. Whenever we intellectualize an experience, it loses its awe and mystery because we have a rational explanation for it. And when that happens, we lose our ability to respond emotionally. I fear the intellectualization of the Pentecostal experience.

These are the things that we must continually bring to the Lord's Table so that holy things never become commonplace to us. We come together often with other believers for the same observance we are celebrating as a group this morning. And today and every time we do this, each of us must endeavor before God not to allow our focus to drift from what we are doing. We must see that bread as *more than bread—* we must see what it represents. As we take the cup, we must also see what *it* represents.

These emblems become holy things because of their purpose, reminding us of the price that was paid for our redemption. We do not believe that the bread becomes the literal body of Christ and the cup becomes the literal blood of Christ. However, if these elements are to mean to us what Christ intended them to mean, *they must be more than bread and more than juice.* We must discern or judge in them the physical body and blood of the Lord.

### The Lord's present Body in the emblems:
### the local church, the district, and the national organization

At another level, holding these emblems in our hands must remind us to rightly judge our local church to be the Lord's Body and, because we are all of the same Body, to examine ourselves regarding any issues that would create distance between and among our members. This is where the independent American spirit gets in the way of Body unity. Most of us want to think of ourselves as individuals who walk with God alone. However, I cannot walk with God *alone*—and neither can you. *"For we are members of his body, of his flesh, and of his bones."*[8] And regardless of where I may see myself fitting into the Body, when that Body becomes divided, it can no longer respond to the Head. And to the extent that one member is divided from the Body, the function of the whole Body becomes impaired. And what of the Body part which is separated from the heart and mind of the Body? Well, it won't live and function very long, will it?

We all are obligated by God to complete a regular self-examination and then take whatever steps are necessary to be properly joined to the Body. If I'm the foot, I can't be joined directly to the head. If I'm an internal organ, I can't be joined directly to the hand. I must be *"fitly joined"*[9] to surrounding members of the Body so that we all may be *"fitly joined"* to the Head, which is Christ. The spirit of independence paralyzes the Body of Christ. The bread and cup remind me that I am joined to every member of my local church, and they are joined to me.

This is also true at the district level. Many times a district-wide effort is weakened by one pastor's pursuit of a selfish vision. A spirit of independence guides that pastor's leadership of the local congregation. Before long a spirit of rebellion creeps in: *I don't care what the district officials think. This is what I'm doing.* That kind of spirit puts distance between us and among us. It weakens us as a body. And if that spirit is brought to the table of the Lord *without being addressed by the person who harbors it,* it will be dealt with by the Lord. If we examine and judge ourselves first, He won't have to call attention to our need. But if we do not judge ourselves, then we will be disciplined by the Lord. We have His Word on that.

And . . . what's true at the district level is also true at the national level. It's amazing, given how much we want our congregation to be united around us, that we can put so much distance between ourselves and our fellow ministers in our district . . . between our district and sister districts . . . between our district and our denominational organization.

### The Lord's present Body extends
### beyond denominational lines

Rightly judging the Lord's Body also requires us to have a right relationship with each other at the extra-denominational level. We need to be in a right relationship with all parts of the Body of Christ. Why? The divisions among us are what render us powerless before the world. They strip from the Church of Jesus Christ the tang we need to really *be* the salt of the earth. The enemy does not fear a large Church. He fears a united Church. For it's only when the members of that Body are properly connected to each other and all of them *"fitly joined"* with the Head that the will of Jesus Christ can be done in our world. This is what Satan fears.

We must ask God to help us keep a sensitive conscience so that when we allow distance to come between us and a brother or sister in Christ the Holy Spirit does not have to hit us with a spiritual "two-by-four" to get our attention. Our hearts need to stay tender before Him so that we can judge ourselves instead of forcing Him to do it.

### The Lord's present Body extends  beyond visible lines

For me personally, rightly judging the Lord's Body at His Table includes reminding myself of my relationship with every member of the Body of Christ who is already with Him—reminding myself of what I owe to those who fought their own *"good fight"* and *"kept the faith."*[10] Whether they are part of our own personal circle of family and friends or former members and pastors of churches where we've served, they now are among that *"great cloud of witnesses"*[11] who are observing how we are running the race and how we are fighting the battle. I don't know about you, but with God's help I want to be found as worthy and as valuable to the Kingdom as they were. I want to examine myself every time I approach the Lord's Table and between times as well, to make sure I am in a right relationship with Him . . . and with all my brothers and sisters in the Body, including those who are now in God's presence.

### The Lord's Body in the ordinances of the church

When Jesus was sharing that very first Communion experience with His disciples after the Feast of the Passover, one of the things He said to them was, *"For as often as ye eat this bread, and drink this cup, ye do shew the Lord's death till he comes."*[12] Notice that it is *as we eat the bread and drink the cup* that we *show* or *bear witness to* the Lord's death until He returns to earth. Those of us among the more iconoclastic portion of the Body of Christ tend to downplay not only *the propriety of religious icons* but also *the importance of many of the ordinances of the Church associated with some of those icons.* We need to know the difference.

In the early days of my ministry, I did not understand the significance of water baptism the way I understand it now. While I do believe that the thief on the cross was with Jesus that very day in paradise, I also believe that water baptism is the way we announce to our community, "I am a Christian." I believe that for those who are physically capable of being immersed in a baptismal tank or other body of water,

water baptism is essential. It was a clear directive, not an optional suggestion, when Jesus said, *"He that believeth and is baptized shall be saved. . . ."*[13] By this symbolic burial and resurrection, we announce to our family, our friends, and our world, "I am dead to my former identity. I am dead to my former self. I am now identified with Jesus Christ."

In my own early days of pastoral ministry, we had no regular time for Communion until God dealt with me about that. I was too busy "proclaiming the gospel." But the gospel is not only proclaimed through preaching. Every time Communion is observed, the gospel is preached, because, *"Ye do shew the Lord's death till he comes."*[14] The emblems we are about to partake of here today are far more than a reminder of what Jesus did for us through His death and resurrection. They also remind the world around us how much God loves them: *"But God commendeth his love toward us, in that, while we were yet sinners, Christ died for us."*[15] Every time we celebrate Communion, we preach a message of salvation. And I like that phrase, *"till He comes."* Here's why.

### The first Adam failed . . . the Second Adam succeeded

God gave the first Adam a mission to populate this planet with others like himself, in order to take control of Earth away from Satan and restore it to God. The first Adam and his mate failed miserably in this mission before they had created even one unfallen human being.

The Second Adam came with another and more complicated mission. First and foremost, He came to give birth to a ransomed, redeemed people, a "race," for lack of a better word, who will occupy this planet for a thousand years. They will rule and reign with Christ and witness Satan's final and everlasting descent into the hell that was prepared for him and his angels. That was the primary mission of Christ—the second Adam—and He did not fail.

Don't think me irreverent when I say Christ did not come primarily to keep us from going to hell, because that is a very self-centered way for us to look at His mission. Christ came to recruit and train God's thousand-year taskforce to put the enemy in his place once and for all. He didn't save us for our personal convenience. God saved you and He saved me because, in His mercy and grace, He counted us among those chosen to rule and reign with Christ for that thousand years on earth!

I personally believe God knows exactly how many sons and daughters He needs to adopt through the new birth in order to subdue this earth and have dominion over it. And whenever the last son or daughter needed to complete that number is reached, we will see the heavens split open as He returns in victory:

> *"For the Lord himself shall descend from heaven with a shout, with the voice of the archangel, and with the trump of God: and the dead in Christ shall rise first: Then we which are alive and remain shall be caught up together with them in the clouds, to meet the Lord in the air: and so shall we ever be with the Lord."*[16]

Because He has deemed His children worthy of sharing in this event, we are coming back with Him to put down forever the rule of Satan. We are coming back to help Him turn the kingdoms of this world into *" . . . the kingdoms of our Lord, and of His Christ; and he shall reign for ever and ever."*[17] Friends, we ought to be far more excited about that whole scenario than just our own individual part in it as we remain faithful to His calling! Hallelujah!

### Giving the Second Adam dominion over our lives

As we partake of these emblems this morning, they are to remind us of our Lord's death. But they are also to remind us that God did not abandon His mission on Earth simply because the first Adam failed. We must learn to see in every observance of Communion that the Second Adam is ever multiplying His forces, preparing to one day subdue and take dominion over this planet. My purpose and your purpose at the Lord's Table this morning is to be sure He has subdued and has dominion over our little part of the planet. We can't help Him increase His forces now or rule earth for a thousand years later on if each of us doesn't give Him control over the four inches between our ears.

It's time for self-examination, right now, at the Table of the Lord. Anything in our lives that challenges His rule needs to be discovered and, with His help, put down. He's here this morning to help us make these kinds of discoveries. So let us examine ourselves . . . so let us eat of the bread and drink of the cup . . . so let us show the Lord's death until His return.

Let's examine our hearts personally and privately now, as we go to the Lord in prayer.

*Father, let Your Holy Spirit have free access to as much of us as we are willing to open to You. And then beyond that, search the parts of us that are not even accessible to us. "Search me, O God, and know my heart: try me, and know my thoughts: And see if there be any wicked way in me, and lead me in the way everlasting."*[18]

*Prepare us this morning to celebrate and enjoy Your blessing at the Table of the Lord because we have judged ourselves and opened those areas of our lives to You that only You can help us straighten out. Having done that, we have cause to celebrate in Jesus' Name. Amen.*

(The emblems of communion are served.)

As we take the bread, let us look to the Lord in prayer.

*Only You, Lord Jesus, know how to make this wafer we hold what it needs to be to each of us. I ask you to take my thoughts back in time and show me again the difference Your broken body made in my life. Remind me of the spirit of rebellion in my heart as a teenager and how different my path is today than it would have been if Your body not been broken for me. Oh, Lord Jesus, I thank You that You were willing to give Your body to be broken so that each of us in the Body of Christ might be made whole.*

*Help us in this moment to allow the Holy Spirit to make us aware of decisions that need to be made and relationships that need to be mended. We don't want to be responsible for distance between and among members of our family, in our local church, in our district, in our movement, or in the Body of Christ. Help us to be joined to one another through Your broken body today. As each of us yields our individual will to Your will, let Your blessing come while we break the bread. Let health come. Let healing flow. Let us feel the blessing You intended to be ours when You were wounded for our transgressions and bruised for our iniquities; when the chastisement of our peace was laid upon You and You bore on Your body the stripes that were for our healing.*[19]

*Let that come to us today throughout this sanctuary as we eat the bread together in Jesus' name. Amen.*

Shall we eat the bread together.

*We truly want to be one in the bonds of love, Lord. We want our spirits to be joined to the Spirit of God in love. Lord, we know that when we say we have no sin in our lives we only deceive ourselves. And I want to be first to confess my sins to You today as I do every day.*

*I ask You for myself and for my brothers and sisters this morning to forgive each of us, Lord, as we each in our own way open those areas of our private lives that need to be cleansed by Your blood. You have said that if we confess our sin, You will be "* . . . faithful and just to forgive us our sins and to cleanse us from all unrighteousness."[20]

*Your Word also tells us that, "* . . . If we walk in the light, as he is in the light, we have fellowship."[21] *There is a wonderful unity when we are one with You and know that the blood of Your Son, Jesus Christ, has cleansed us from all our sin. Cleanse me. Cleanse each of us today, Lord Jesus, through Your precious blood as we drink the cup together. In Jesus' Name we pray. Amen.*

Shall we partake of the cup together.

---

[1] NOTE: Dolores went to be with the Lord a few weeks after this message was delivered. Some time later, God brought another wonderful woman into my life—I have been doubly blessed! I am now happily married to the former Priscilla Adams of Lafayette, Indiana.

[2] 1 Corinthians 11:17-34 (NASB).
[3] Matthew 25:21.
[4] 1 Corinthians 10:16,17 (NASB).
[5] 1 Corinthians 1:10-13.
[6] 1 Corinthians 9:24-27.
[7] 1 Corinthians 11:28,29.
[8] Ephesians 5:30.
[9] Ephesians 4:16
[10] 2 Timothy 4:7.
[11] Hebrews 11:1-12:1.
[12] 1 Corinthians 11:26.
[13] Mark 16:16.

[14] 1 Corinthians 11:26.
[15] Romans 5:8.
[16] 1 Thessalonians 4:16,17.
[17] Revelation 11:15.
[18] Psalm 139:23,24.
[19] Isaiah 53:5.
[20] 1 John 1:9.
[21] 1 John 1:7.

# 9

# The Tent, the Treasure, & the Tenant *

What a joy it is to be here with all of you and to serve the Lord together. Brother Crabtree and Brother McManness have been my dear friends for many, many years. It's an honor for me to have been included among their friends and to have worked together with them on so many district projects. Seeing our Presbytery Board here this morning I am reminded of the years of dedicated Christian service they represent and the wonderful fellowship that we enjoy. Our district has never been more unified at the leadership level, and that's something I think we need to celebrate.

As most of you know, my wife, Dolores, has gone to be with the Lord since I ministered to you last year. This is the first time I've assumed this responsibility without the support of her earthly prayers. Not only do I believe that the saints in heaven are praying, but I would be very discouraged if I thought the success of the church depended only on the prayer life of the saints on earth!

I remember saying to Dolores one evening, when it was looking like her homegoing was close at hand, "Honey, you know how heavily I've counted on your prayers. When you're there in the presence of the Lord, don't forget to pray for me." And she laughed, and said, "You silly thing! If I've prayed for you here on earth, when I don't even know how desperately I should be praying, how much more do you think I'll be praying for you when I'm in the presence of the Lord and know how much you really do need my prayers!"

---

* Sermon for the Communion Service of the 1993 Ohio District Council of the Assemblies of God, Tri County Assembly of God, Fairfield, Ohio.

And now let's get into our message this morning.

*"For we do not preach ourselves but Christ Jesus as Lord, and ourselves as your bond-servants for Jesus' sake. For God, who said, 'Light shall shine out of darkness,' is the One who has shone in our hearts to give the light of the knowledge of the glory of God in the face of Christ.*

*"But we have this treasure in earthen vessels, that the surpassing greatness of the power may be of God and not from ourselves; we are afflicted in every way, but not crushed; perplexed, but not despairing; persecuted, but not forsaken; struck down, but not destroyed; always carrying about in the body the dying of Jesus, that the life of Jesus also may be manifested in our body.*

*"For we who live are constantly being delivered over to death for Jesus' sake, that the life of Jesus also may be manifested in our mortal flesh. So death works in us, but life in you. But having the same spirit of faith, according to what is written, 'I BELIEVED, THEREFORE I SPOKE,' we also believe, therefore also we speak; knowing that He who raised the Lord Jesus will raise us also with Jesus and will present us with you. For all things are for your sakes, that the grace which is spreading to more and more people may cause the giving of thanks to abound to the glory of God.*

*"Therefore we do not lose heart, but though our outer man is decaying, yet our inner man is being renewed day by day. For momentary, light affliction is producing for us an eternal weight of glory far beyond all comparison, while we look not at the things which are seen, but at the things which are not seen; for the things which are seen are temporal, but the things which are not seen are eternal.*

*"For we know that if the earthly tent which is our house is torn down, we have a building from God, a house not made with hands, eternal in the heavens. For indeed in this house we groan, longing to be clothed with our dwelling from heaven; inasmuch as we, having put it on, shall not be found naked. For indeed while we are in this tent, we groan, being burdened,*

*because we do not want to be unclothed, but to be clothed, in order that what is mortal may be swallowed up by life.*

*"Now He who prepared us for this very purpose is God, who gave to us the Spirit as a pledge. Therefore, being always of good courage, and knowing that while we are at home in the body, we are absent from the Lord—for we walk by faith, not by sight—we are of good courage, I say, and prefer rather to be absent from the body and to be at home with the Lord. Therefore also we have as our ambition, whether at home or absent, to be pleasing to Him. For we must all appear before the judgment seat of Christ, that each one may be recompensed for his deeds in the body, according to what he has done, whether good or bad."*[1]

I want to focus on just a few words from this passage: *"But we have this treasure in earthen vessels, that the surpassing greatness of the power may be of God and not from ourselves."*[2]

Shall we bow our hearts in prayer.

*Father, we're about to approach the Table of Your Son and our Lord. We are about to hold in our hands what He asked us to hold as a memorial and a reminder of His death. I ask this morning that You anoint us all to say what You would have us say and hear what You would have us hear. For only then can we expect to see done what You want to be done in us and to us and through us. We commit ourselves to You this morning and pray that You will speak to us through Your Word and by Your Spirit, that Communion today might be a special time for each of us in our journey with You. In Jesus' name we pray, Amen.*

Throughout her battle with cancer, Dolores focused more and more on these verses. They became her very favorite passage of Scripture. In her devotional times, she read from these chapters again and again. And in her final weeks, she listened to these verses from audio tapes of the New Testament that someone was kind enough to give her. The last few days of her life on earth, I often read these verses to her—not even knowing at times how much she could hear. As I shared the final miles of her earthly journey with her to the best of my ability, I learned some unforgettable lessons about the *tent,* the *treasure,* and the *tenant.* I'd like to share those with you today.

## God has given each of us a "tent"

First of all, let's take a look at the tent. *"For we know that if the earthly tent which is our house is torn down, we have a building from God, a house not made with hands, eternal in the heavens."*[3]

Sometimes I think we place too little value on our earthly tent, the human body God created to house His glory on earth. Some Bible scholars have suggested that Adam and Eve were originally clothed with God's glory, and that *the loss of that glory* is what made them aware of their own nakedness. A body void of God's glory is at best a life without eternal worth and meaning; a life under the curse of sin.

Trying to fill the body with anything less than God's glory is to deny the ultimate meaning of the body. Paul reminds us that, *"the body is . . . for the Lord; and the Lord is for the body."*[4] When Adam rejected God's ownership of his body, God promised He would create another body. In Genesis 3:15 (NASB), we see the first Messianic promise of the Scripture: *"And I will put enmity between you and the woman, And between your seed and her seed; He shall bruise you on the head, And you shall bruise him on the heel."* In reminding us of that day when this promise was fulfilled, the writer says in Hebrews 10:5 (NASB), *"Therefore, when He comes into the world, He says, 'SACRIFICE AND OFFERING THOU HAST NOT DESIRED, BUT A BODY THOU HAST PREPARED FOR ME.'"*

We can never make a sacrifice that is adequate to compensate for our disobedience. God wants from us bodies who will obey His will. He will never accomplish *through what we give Him* what can only be accomplished by *what He wants to do through us.* Someone, somewhere, sometime, has said, "Your life is God's gift to you. What you make of it is your gift to Him."

## We are to serve Him in our tent

John reminds us that the physical, earthly body that was prepared for Jesus was filled with the glory of God: *"And the Word became flesh, and dwelt among us, and we beheld His glory, glory as of the only begotten from the Father, full of grace and truth."*[5] I would remind us this morning, my friends, that Communion is about Christ's body, prepared to house God's glory.

Jesus himself said the emblems that we will soon take in our hands—the Bread and the Cup—are to remind us of His body: *"This is my body which is given for you . . . This cup is the new testament in my blood, which is shed for you."*[6] These emblems are to remind us of Christ's sacrificial and atoning death for our sins. They are to remind us of His triumphant power over death, hell, and the grave. They are to remind us of His resurrection and ascension into heaven where He now intercedes for us. They are to remind us that He who is gone will come again—and that when He does, we will sit with Him around the Table.

In the glow of that glorious moment, there will be a time of heart-searching when, just as He confronted the disciples during the first Lord's Supper, He will ask each of us how much of our tent we have shared with Him. For Communion is not only about His earthly body; it's about your body and about my body. It's about a loving God, rejected by His creation, Who reaches out again through Christ to redeem the human body as a temple for His glory.

*"What? know ye not that your body is the temple of the Holy Ghost which is in you, which ye have of God, and ye are not your own? For ye are bought with a price: therefore glorify God in your body, and in your spirit, which are God's."*[7] Any purpose to which we devote this tent other than to the glory of God desecrates His temple. Yes, it's a tent; its existence is transient; but, while it is on earth, it is intended to house the glory of God. We need to take good care of it so that we may present it to Him as a living sacrifice without having to be ashamed of what we've done to it or through it.[8]

### What kind of treasure is housed in the tent?

Now let's focus for a few moments on the treasure that each of us has in our personal tent, for it's the treasure that gives worth to the tent. On its own, the tent isn't worth very much. But when it is serving the purpose God intended it to serve, housing the treasure He intended it to house, then it is very valuable.

Paul says the treasure housed in our tent is the radiant *"light of the knowledge of the glory of God"*[9] as seen in the face of Jesus Christ. That light can be a little overwhelming the first time it shines toward our personal darkness. The Bethlehem shepherds didn't know what to think of *"the glory of the Lord"* that *"shone around them; and they were terribly frightened"* until they'd been to the manger and come face to face with its source.[10] It was there they realized the transforming power of God, as they saw His glory reflected in the face of the infant Jesus. They went back to their life and work with a new treasure stored up inside their personal tents, singing praises to God for what they had experienced. They were transformed by the glory of God.

God's glory still has the power to transform us, just as it forever changed the Bethlehem shepherds. Paul closes the third chapter of 2 Corinthians on that very note: *"But we all, with unveiled face beholding as in a mirror the glory of the Lord, are being transformed into the same image from glory to glory, just as from the Lord, the Spirit (NASB)."*

The tent is possessed by the treasure through revelation and experience. These are two ways of *knowing* that the world often disdains, but they are the primary ways by which we come to know God. We cannot acquire the glory of God by education. We cannot acquire the glory of God by indoctrination. His glory comes by revelation and experience. *"But the natural man receiveth not the things of the Spirit of God: for they are foolish unto him: neither can he know them, because they are spiritually discerned."*[11]

As I have opportunity, I share the three things I fear for our fellowship as I look back upon my life in the Assemblies of God and anticipate what may face us in the next two or three decades. I know I've already mentioned them at district gatherings like this one, but I'm going to share this particular concern with you again.

First of all, I fear the *institutionalization* of our church. This seems to be a process all of us recognize but none of us can stop.

Second, I fear the *professionalization* of the ministry where by seniority we claim our right to larger churches; where by education we claim our right to fringe benefits; where we so unwisely compare ourselves to ourselves and measure ourselves by ourselves instead of making those comparisons and measurements against the Word of God.

Third, I fear the *intellectualization* of the Pentecostal experience. I'm troubled by the fact that so few people receive the Baptism in the

Holy Spirit at the altars of our churches. And I'm troubled by the way we accommodate this trend; by seeing that some special emphasis is placed upon it at boys' camp, girls' camp, youth camp, men's conventions, and women's conventions. I'm glad to know people receive the Baptism in the Holy Spirit at these special functions, but I have to ask myself why so many are experiencing it there and so few are receiving this gift around our altars. Are *we* unwilling to take the time to minister to this need in people's lives? Are *the people of our congregations* too busy to spend time seeking this experience? Or do we—or they—*no longer understand its importance* in the believer's life?

### God wants us to experience His presence every day

We are a movement born out of revelation and experience. God wills to reveal himself to us. He wants us to experience His presence. Additionally, God wills that these revelations of himself and these experiences of His presence accumulate and multiply in a sort of geometric proportion in our lives.

In 2 Corinthians 3:18 (NASB) we discover that during our lifelong walk with Christ, *". . . We all, with unveiled face beholding as in a mirror the glory of the Lord, are being transformed into the same image from glory to glory, just as from the Lord, the Spirit."* There is a *cumulative* impression created by Paul's words here and confirmed in 2 Corinthians 4:17 (NASB), where he says, *"For momentary, light affliction is producing for us an eternal weight of glory far beyond all comparison."* From cumulative encounters with *"light affliction"* comes the abundance or *"weight"* of glory. It is the treasure of this revelation and experience that shines out through the good works of our lives and bears witness to those with whom we work and live, to bring glory to our heavenly Father.

These are not good works for good works' sake; they are the irrepressible, joyful, natural expression of our intense awareness of Christ's presence in our lives. Christ went about doing good everywhere He went, by virtue of who He was. Likewise, whenever we have the opportunity, as *". . . partakers of the [same] divine nature . . . "*[12] we are to *". . . do good to all men, and especially to those who are of the household of the faith,"*[13] so that, *". . . they might see [our] good works, and glorify [our] Father who is in heaven.*"[14] Why is this so important? Because these residual *"good works"* produced in us by the revelation of Christ are the only parts of our lives that will survive the final trial by fire[15] that evaluates the strength of our faith while we are here on earth.

Scripture clearly tells us that, *"We must all appear before the judgment seat of Christ; that every one may receive the things done in his body, according to that he hath done, whether it be good or bad."*[16] What will happen at this moment of judgment?

> *"Now if any man builds upon the foundation with gold, silver, precious stones, wood, hay, straw, each man's work will become evident; for the day will show it, because it is to be revealed with fire; and the fire itself will test the quality of each man's work. If any man's work which he has built upon it remains, he shall receive a reward. If any man's work is burned up, he shall suffer loss; but he himself shall be saved, yet so as through fire."*[17]

The wood, hay, and stubble of the things we've done to accomplish our own ends will vanish in that moment in the fire. Only the divine, cumulative residual of our earthly pilgrimage—our time in the tent—will remain. Is it any wonder, then, that Paul admonishes us, *"For no man can lay a foundation other than the one which is laid, which is Jesus Christ."*[18]

Over the last eleven months since Dolores went to be with the Lord, I've had a lot of time to think about the way she lived her Christian life. She had this kind of "cumulative" faith. I knew her better than I've ever known any other human being. She was a wonderful wife and passionate lover, and the most godly woman I have ever known. She accumulated an experience of the glory of God that was obvious to me, our children, and everyone else who knew her well enough to make such an observation. Her treasure and her heart were in service to her Lord.

Now, finally, let's take a look at the tenant. For each of us have the awesome responsibility and the exciting opportunity to choose the life—the treasure—that will be housed in and manifested from our tent. We must never forget that we are in a lifelong battle over whose treasure we will house and display.

## Choosing the treasure for the tent

Every day of my life, every day of your life, the enemy is hard at work enticing us with his thoughts and suggestions, tempting us to give expression to his presence in our body. At the same time, through His Word and by His Spirit, God is continually inviting us to a new experience—a new revelation—of His Son Jesus Christ, so that we might have and express the life and love of Christ through our bodies. By the grace of God, we are free to choose whether we will give expression to God's enemy or to His Son, Jesus Christ. With that freedom to choose comes the consequences of our choice. And this *is* a matter of personal choice. Just like the Israelites of Joshua's day, we choose which master we will serve.[20]

This is the basis of Paul's plea in Romans 12:1: *"I beseech you therefore, brethren, by the mercies of God, that ye present your bodies a living sacrifice, holy, acceptable unto God, which is your reasonable service."*

I want to make room for Him in my tent; to treasure the revelation of Christ that God has given me; to resist the pressures of the world to fit into its materialistic mold. Instead of conforming to this world, I want to allow God by the revelation of His presence through His Son to transform me and conform me to Christ's image.

## Becoming a godly tenant

What does a godly tenant do with his or her body? First of all, a godly tenant serves God and others. *" . . . My earnest expectation and my hope,"* Paul prays in Philippians 1:20 that, *" . . . Christ shall be magnified in my body, whether it be by life, or by death."* Psalm 40:6 explains what God *doesn't* want from His people: *"Sacrifice and offering thou didst not desire . . . burnt offering and sin offering hast thou not required."* The writer to the Hebrews uses different words to express this same thought and even take it a little further. *" . . . Sacrifice and offering thou wouldest not, but a body hast thou prepared me: In burnt offerings and sacrifices for sin thou hast had no pleasure."*[21] Not only does God not *require* burnt offerings and sacrifices for sin, He doesn't even *want* them. He simply wants tenants willing to house His treasure in the bodies He has provided for that purpose. If we don't invite Him into our lives to be expressed through our bodies, it won't matter how many sacrifices and burnt offerings we make. He won't be impressed.

Christ was not only our once-and-for-all sin offering and sacrifice; He also set the example for us. He showed us the kind of tenant God wants in each human tent. This is what the Holy Spirit seems to be saying in Hebrews 9:26,28: "*. . . now once . . . hath he appeared to put away sin by the sacrifice of himself . . . Christ was once offered to bear the sins of many . . . .*" As the tenant of His earthly body, Jesus took control and presented His life in loving service to His heavenly Father. In much the same way that the bond slave had his ear pierced and a ring put through it to show his gratitude to his master, Jesus presented His body to the Father as His loving servant. How can we do anything less and call ourselves by His Name?

As we begin to live a life of service, we discover the paradox of this lifestyle: the only way to maximize the harvest of your life is to fall into the ground of God's will and die to your own selfish desires. We're like that grain of corn or wheat that brings forth its great potential harvest only after it falls into the ground and dies. The godly tenant serves by dying to self and living to serve others.

### Godly tenants sacrifice themselves for others

Dolores taught me far more about sacrifice than I ever taught her. It was not unusual for her to use money gifts from me or from our children to help needy people in the church buy groceries. Our family remembers her as one who inspired us through her ministry of sacrificial giving to others. I think all of us are aware this is a diminishing ministry among us today. And yet godly tenants not only *serve;* they *sacrifice* for the Master. They don't *bring* a sacrifice; they *are* a living sacrifice. Their lives are spent in the service of their Lord.

We tend to think of something being *spent* only in the sense of money exchanged for goods or services. But in the context we're talking about here, to be *spent* means to have used up all of one's time, energy, and other resources in pursuing some goal. A champion runner is *spent* when he or she falls on the ground, unable to move, at the end of the marathon. There are no resources left on which to draw. This is the way we are to *spend* ourselves in service to our heavenly Father.

### Godly tenants need a theology of suffering

Godly tenants suffer. *We need a theology of suffering.* Don't misunderstand me. We believe God heals people in His own time and for His own purposes—to provide visible evidence that Jesus is the Christ. We believe healings will continue to serve as *"signs following"* the preaching of the gospel message until our Lord returns. We also know that until He does return, the vast majority of us will leave this world through the process of disease.

This is why Paul says we wait, *". . . to wit, for the redemption of our bodies."*[22] And that little clause we so often brush past, *"to wit,"* is an interesting phrase. One of the (now rather archaic) meanings of "wit" is *the ability to relate apparently disparate things to each other to bring illumination to something that had been unclear.* In other words, it's the ability to put a spiritual two-and-two together—and come out with four. *How well prepared we are to accept our means of exit from this world when it comes* speaks to how well we have been able to relate our *present suffering* to the *eventual redemption* of our bodies. It speaks to our godliness. It's what happens when by faith we arrive at the realization that no matter how we may suffer in this world, our suffering is only *"a light affliction, which is but for a moment,"*[23] when compared to the joy of finally being at home for eternity with our Lord.

God's people need a clear theology of suffering—especially those who are in traditional Pentecostal and charismatic circles. When anointing with oil or the laying-on of hands and prayer do not bring healing, many in this part of the Body of Christ blame themselves. "There must be sin in my life or God would heal me." Others question God's love. "Why doesn't He heal me? He healed Sister So-and-So. Why not me?"

Don't misunderstand me here; we need to read about the heroes of faith catalogued for us in Hebrews chapter 11, those who were delivered from impossible situations *"by faith."* This is one of our sources of strength during dark days. We need to know we serve a God of miracles. *But what about the others mentioned later on in that same chapter?* They were tortured, they suffered cruel mockings and beatings, they were imprisoned, stoned, sawn asunder, tempted, and slain with the sword. They were left to wander around clothed in animal skins. They were destitute, afflicted, and tormented. Alone in the deserts and the mountains, many lived in dens and caves of the earth like animals.

We hear very little about this group, and yet they all died *"in the faith."* They didn't die because someone didn't fast long enough. They didn't die because someone's faith fell short. They didn't die because God wasn't powerful enough or didn't care enough to perform a miracle. They died the way they died because *not everyone who serves God is healed of every physical affliction.*

Not all believers were healed even when Jesus walked the earth. He did not empty every village of all its afflicted. John 5:1-11 tells us He healed one person among the *"great multitude"* at the Pool at Bethesda who were *". . . blind, halt, withered . . .."* They were all there, waiting for the angel of God to ripple the waters as a sign that there was healing for—how many?—the *first person* to step into the pool. One person. They knew what we have somehow forgotten: God never promised that everybody who comes to Him for healing will be healed. Jesus didn't break with God's established tradition that day, although He fulfilled it in a new and unique way. He still healed just one among the many who sought healing.

And He healed that man for the same reason God always heals: to bring people to an awareness of His power and grace. That doesn't mean we shouldn't seek healing, for Scripture clearly directs us to do just that.[24] But it does mean we may not be healed during our human lifetime. So, while we do not ever want to lessen our emphasis on healing, we also don't want to leave those saints of God who are suffering without some way of explaining their suffering to themselves—a theology of suffering—that helps them see it in light of eternity.

I didn't realize the level of courage God had given Dolores for dealing with the terrible pain she would encounter as she prepared to enter His presence. She didn't consider herself to be a very courageous person. She wasn't a risk-taker. She was a pain-avoidant person—as most of us are, if we're honest about it. But in her battle with cancer, I never once heard her complain. At times she would say to me, at night, "I just wish I could go to sleep and wake up in heaven." But she didn't complain about her physical pain.

True saints know how to suffer with grace. One's character surfaces during times of suffering, the character developed in them over time by that cumulative presence of whatever master they've chosen to serve in their earthly tent. It was not hard to tell that Dolores had served the living God, because she displayed an amazing awareness of His presence and His grace through her suffering. At times she surprised even those of us who knew her best, resting in God beyond all our human understanding.

### Godly tenants celebrate
### the life God gives them

Godly tenants celebrate life every step of the way. I watched Dolores struggle with the limitations of her physical life in her final days. In ministering to other grieving families I had observed the death of many saints of God. However, I had never before had to give this depth of thought to what goes on when a saint of God dies. I was brought face to face with the process.

Dolores was only confined to the upstairs of our home for the last two weeks of her life on earth. Until two weeks before she went to be with the Lord, she fixed breakfast for me every morning. As her physical condition drained more and more of her strength, our meals became more simple—but she also still fixed dinner for me every night. Our routines for doing even the easiest of tasks helped both of us celebrate every moment that we were still together, even as we became more and more aware of the change that was about to take place in both our lives.

When she was eventually confined upstairs, those who tended her were amazed at how little relief she still needed from pain. She was able to *rest* in her relationship with Jesus and was spared the half-life of drug-induced pain relief much of the time. She was only confined to her bed five days. On Saturday her condition took a decided turn for the worse. By Monday, she was in the presence of Jesus.

Our daughter, Sharon, lives in Connecticut. She had just gone home on Saturday. When she called Dolores early Sunday, one of the first things she said to her was, "Mom, you sound so much weaker today."

Dolores responded to her by saying, "Well, honey, I'm closer to heaven today."

Sharon answered, "Mom, you remember—you promised that you'd let me know if you thought you were going to go so I could come home and have some more quality time with you."

Dolores answered back, "Well, honey, Ramsey [our son-in-law] has been so good to let you come so often. You're coming Thursday; just wait 'til Thursday."

And Sharon reminded her again, "Now, Mom, remember you promised me that you wouldn't slip into unconsciousness without giving me some quality time."

Dolores said, "Well, honey, you'd better come tomorrow." Sharon got in the car and came home from Connecticut *that day.*

I never will forget her pulling into the driveway and looking up at the bedroom window. I'd heard the noise in the driveway and anticipated it being her. I watched her get out of the car and then stood at the top of the stairs, watching her come up. That was the first night the hospice worker was spending the night in our home.

I slept downstairs on the daybed that night. Sharon spent the night in the room with her mother, and that was Dolores' last night of full consciousness. It was a very special time for Sharon, and she has wonderful memories of those last few hours with her mother.

By caring for Dolores at home, the family was there during the whole process of her leave-taking. I watched her struggle deep within her spirit, as she would moan and groan in communication with her Lord, when she would be dealing with the uncertainty of what was going to happen next in her physical body; whether she would remain able to sense God's presence with her during the difficult days ahead.

She wasn't afraid of what lay on the other side of the death process. She knew that being *there* would be better than being *here* even on the best day of her earthly life. But, like most of us, she was uneasy about some of the process that would get her from here to there and she was communing with God about this at very deep levels of her spirit.

During those days, 2 Corinthians 5:1-10 became very real to me. Although none of us will have our resurrected body until Christ returns, He has made provision for what Paul called the *clothing of our spirit.* We have the assurance that our spirit *"shall not be found naked;"*

in other words, that it is reassured or clothed by the goodness of God here on earth until *"what is mortal [is] swallowed up by life."*[25]

### " . . . Through the valley of the shadow of death . . . "

As Dolores became comfortable knowing that the Shepherd was there to lead her through that place we know as *"the valley of the shadow of death,"*[26] a peace came into her spirit that all of us were aware of. It was only the *shadow* of death, *not death itself*, that would touch her, for her life was secure in God's hands.

Early in the morning of the day Dolores died, the hospice worker told us her fingers were turning blue and there was a lot of moisture in her breathing; she was going to slip away from us very soon. We gathered around her bed, and read this passage from 2 Corinthians 5. Sharon read Romans 8. And then we sang: "Amazing Grace;" "My Jesus, I Love Thee;" "We Are Standing On Holy Ground;" "Mansion Over the Hilltop;" "What a Day That Will Be."

While the nurses changed shifts, we went downstairs for some breakfast. Less than five minutes later, the nurse came to tell us Dolores had passed into the presence of the Lord. While I can tell you we were sad, we were not depressed. We had known the time of her departure was at hand. She had fought her good fight. She had finished her course. She had kept the faith. That outward man that had been perishing day by day[27] was now just a vacated tent. But inwardly she had been *"renewed day by day."*[28] The tenant and the treasure were gone from the tent to spend eternity with the Lord Whom she had loved and served, for Whom she had lived and sacrificed. She would never again know pain or experience sorrow. It was a moving experience for our family.

Not one of us here this morning knows the time or the circumstances by which we will make the transition into the presence of our Lord. And although we will never face His judgment for our sins, we *will* see Him sift our works to determine which of them are of worth to the Kingdom. We want that to be a time of celebration as we lay those works that have survived at His feet.

It is for this reason we pray now, as we approach the Table . . .

*Let our earthly tents be filled with the treasure of the transforming glory of God as we learn to spend our life for You by serving*

*You and serving others. Help us remember that being absent from the body means being present with You. And in that day when we stand in Your presence, we want to be able to lay some divinely inspired works of gold, silver, and precious jewels at Your feet. We don't want to bring only wood, hay, and stubble. We want to be good stewards of the tent You have given us.*

*Teach us to be godly tenants who serve You and those You bring into our lives. Help us learn how to sacrifice for Your glory, not our own. Help us learn how to show Your presence even in our suffering. And show us how to celebrate every moment of the life You've given us.*

*We're all aware that we are not our own; we've been bought with a price. We are so grateful that even when we spurned You in creation, Your redemptive love persisted and gave us another chance to let Your glory reside in us. You sent Your written and Living Word to show us how to be partakers of Your divine nature.*

*This morning as we gather around Your table and hold in our hands emblems of Your body, remind us, Lord of how the stewardship of our bodies is transacted day by day in our tent. Help us to pray with John the Baptist,* "He must increase and I must decrease," *until we can honestly say, as Paul said, that* "For me to live is for Christ to live." *In Jesus' Name we pray, Amen.*

The brethren are going to come now and prepare to serve us the emblems. And as you receive them in your hands, just hold the emblems and we'll pray over each one before we partake of them together.

(Congregational singing: "See His Glory Come Down.")

*Father, we hold in our hands today the emblem of Your Son's broken body. Lord Jesus, we pause to reflect on the fact that we can never know what it's like for sinlessness to be made sin; to know what it's like for One who is righteous and innocent to suffer for those who are sinful and guilty. Your earthly tent was enough like ours for You to be tempted in all points like as we are, and yet Your tent was enough like the heavenly Father to be without sin.*

*We don't understand that mystery of godliness that allowed God to be made manifest in human flesh, but we thank You, Lord Jesus, that*

*You who spoke the worlds into existence became one of us; became sin for us that we might be made the righteousness of God. As we prepare to take this bread this morning, may those who are sick recognize in the bread the stripes that were borne upon Your back for our healing. And may they find in it the strength to bear up under suffering until healing comes. For You were not only bruised, Lord Jesus; You suffered; and You're with us in our sufferings. You're with us in our sicknesses. We pray that You will be glorified in our body, whether by our life or by our death.*

*Let our life be so exemplary of Your presence that for us to live on this earth is for You to live on this earth as we show Your love to those around us. A we eat of the bread, may Your Body become to each of us what we individually need this morning. In Jesus' Name we pray, Amen.*

Shall we eat together.

*Lord Jesus, we hold in our hand the cup, representing Your blood shed for the remission of sins ... a new covenant God made with us that doesn't rest on the blood of bulls and goats; but the blood of a spotless Lamb . . . hallelujah! . . . shed for us . . . confident that if we are honest enough to confess our sins, You are faithful and just to forgive us our sins and to cleanse us from all unrighteousness. I join with my brothers and sisters this morning in confessing my sins to You, Lord Jesus. Come in a way that only You can come to cleanse me, Lord. Cleanse me and I shall be whiter than snow. As we drink together, Lord, may we be conscious that our sins are being washed away from us as far as the east is from the west. And may we celebrate that freshness, that new-found innocence of being able to stand without condemnation before You, Lord. In Jesus' Name we pray, Amen.*

Let's drink together, and then let's lift our voices in praise to the Lord for His love and grace.

---

[1] 2 Corinthians 4:5-5:10, NASB.
[2] 2 Corinthians 4:7, NASB.
[3] 2 Corinthians 5:1, NASB.

[4] 1 Corinthians 6:13, NASB.
[5] John 1:14, NASB.
[6] Luke 22:19,20.
[7] 1 Corinthians 6:19,20.
[8] Romans 12:1.
[9] 2 Corinthians 4:6, NASB.
[10] Luke 2:8-20, NASB.
[11] 1 Corinthians 2:14.
[12] 2 Peter 1:4, NASB.
[13] Galatians 6:10, NASB.
[14] Matthew 5:16, NASB.
[15] 1 Corinthians 3:13.
[16] 2 Corinthians 5:10.
[17] 1 Corinthians 3:12-15, NASB.
[18] 1 Corinthians 3:11, NASB.
[19] Luke 12:34.
[20] Joshua 24:15.
[21] Hebrews 10:5,6.
[22] Romans 8:23.
[23] 2 Corinthians 4:17.
[24] James 5:16.
[25] 2 Corinthians 5:3,4, NASB.
[26] Psalm 23:4.
[27] 2 Corinthians 4:16.
[28] Ibid.

# 10

# Your Body: Evidence of Spiritual Tragedy or Triumph? *

Following Dolores' homegoing in June, 1992, I was so overwhelmed with grief that I never thought of a future with anyone else. However, some time ago, the Lord indicated to me that it wasn't His will for me to live the rest of my life as a single person. I was very, very anxious about the process of dating and finding someone with whom to share my life. It's a lot different to be thinking along those lines at this stage of life than it is when you're a college-age young adult. Of course, the principles of forming a healthy love relationship remain the same for any age candidate. I went back and read my own booklet, "Narrowing the Risk in Mate Selection." I have to tell you that I have a new perspective on that now!

I'm very grateful to God for using the good pastors at First Assembly in Lafayette, Indiana, to bring Priscilla and me together. And we're both very grateful to God for the life He is giving us. We ask for your prayers that God will keep us where He wants us to be and use us for His honor and His glory.

I'm always a bit anxious as I approach our Wednesday morning Communion service at District Council. I've done this for so many years now that I'm sometimes afraid it will lose some of the uniqueness that is so important to this service. I hope the ink is dry by now on this morning's notes. I've asked God to give me a message that will be fresh to me as well as to you, because we all need a totally fresh touch from Him.

Our Scripture reading this morning is from Luke's account of that first Communion service:

---

* Sermon for the Communion Service of the 1994 Ohio District Council of the Assemblies of God, Highway Tabernacle, Youngstown, Ohio.

113

*"And when the hour had come He reclined at table, and the apostles with Him. And He said to them, 'I have earnestly desired to eat this Passover with you before I suffer; for I say to you, I shall never again eat it until it is fulfilled in the kingdom of God.'*

*"And having taken a cup, when He had given thanks, He said, 'Take this and share it among yourselves; for I say to you, I will not drink of the fruit of the vine from now on until the kingdom of God comes.' And having taken some bread, when He had given thanks, He broke it, and gave it to them, saying, 'This is My body which is given for you; do this in remembrance of Me.' And in the same way, He took the cup after they had eaten, saying, 'This cup which is poured out for you is the new covenant in My blood.*

*"'But behold, the hand of the one betraying Me is with Me on the table. For indeed, the Son of Man is going as it has been determined; but woe to that man through whom He is betrayed!'"*[1]

Shall we bow our hearts in prayer.

*Father, we thank You for making us body persons. Every time we see a baby born into this world, we are reminded that human life is indeed a miracle. When we address You as Father, we remember Who is responsible for the mystery of life. We pray this morning, as we gather at Your Table—laborers in Your work—that You will help us realize anew the miracle of our own human life. Help us never to lose the sense of awe that the human body evokes. Help us to be good stewards of our body. In Jesus' Name we pray, Amen.*

The distance between the most limited of human beings and the most intelligent creature of the ape family is not a missing *link;* it's a missing *leap.* Humans were the only element of creation identified by Scripture as having been made in the image of God, after His own likeness.[2] Of all that God created, humanity alone is uniquely made in His image. This suggests that human bodies on this planet are called to serve a special purpose. It is a purpose no other kind of being on earth can fulfill. There is nothing else like us on this planet.

Because our human bodies are the only life we have ever known, sometimes I think we take the miracle of the body for granted. David, however, never lost his awe of mankind. That sense of wonder is apparent in David's eighth Psalm:

> *"When I consider Thy heavens, the work of Thy fingers, The moon and the stars, which Thou hast ordained; What is man, that Thou doest take thought of him? And the son of man, that Thou dost care for him? Yet Thou hast made him a little lower than God, and dost crown him with glory and majesty! Thou dost make him to rule over the works of Thy hands; Thou hast put all things under his feet."*[3]

So simply but eloquently put in this passage, the purpose of the human body is to house the presence of God on earth and to restore divine dominion over this rebellious planet. Let me say that again: the purpose of the human body is to house the presence of God on earth and to restore divine dominion over this rebellious planet.

Notice that the emphasis is on the body. Had God not wanted to make us body persons, He could have created us *spirit beings*, without bodies. But He chose to make us body persons. The human body was uniquely created to house God's presence on earth and restore His dominion over this planet. This is the thought I trust will capture our hearts this morning.

### The tragedy of the first Adam's body

First of all, let's take a look at *the tragedy of Adam's body* as a means of helping restore this planet to the Creator. In Genesis 2:7, Moses says that the human body was created as an urn to house God's presence on earth. He says God formed man of the dust of the ground and breathed a part of himself into that unique urn He had fashioned to house His presence.

What this means, friends, is that until His presence is being expressed in my body, my body is being denied its highest purpose. Let me repeat that, for it's an important concept and central to the rest of the message this morning. Until God's presence finds expression in my body, my body is being denied the divine purpose for which it was created.

## We are created to house God's presence

This is the tragedy of the human family today. In the cities where we pastor, in the towns and villages where we labor, every human being has the capacity through God's grace to house His presence in his or her body. For the period of time that one's body is *without* God's presence, that body is being denied its highest purpose. It is being prostituted for a lesser use.

Genesis 2:25 infers that before the fall, Adam and Eve were so covered with the glory of God in their bodies that they were unaware of their nakedness. In the Scripture portion we read earlier, David reminds us that man was made only *"a little lower"* than God. Adam and Eve were bodily expressions of God's glory; it literally clothed them.

Let's turn to Genesis 2:7 (NASB) and read about the creation of the first human: *"Then the Lord God formed man of dust from the ground, and breathed into his nostrils the breath of life; and man became a living being."*

Now let's go to Genesis 3:7-11 (NASB), after Eve's creation, and after they had succumbed to the serpent's temptation:

> *"Then the eyes of both of them were opened, and they knew that they were naked; and they sewed fig leaves together and made themselves loin coverings. And they heard the sound of the Lord God walking in the garden in the cool of the day, and the man and his wife hid themselves from the presence of the Lord God among the trees of the garden. Then the Lord God called to the man, and said to him, 'Where are you?' And he said, 'I heard the sound of thee in the garden, and I was afraid because I was naked; so I hid myself.' And He said, 'Who told you that you were naked?'"*

Disobedience had stripped Adam and Eve of the glory of God and made them aware of their nakedness. Their disobedience to God denied each of their bodies its highest purpose. And when we get to the bottom of our own personal misery, my friends, that is the story.

The solution to our problem is found in that simple formula penned by the hymnwriter and Presbyterian minister J. H. Sammis: "Trust and Obey." His words came directly out of a testimony given in one of

Dwight L. Moody's services in 1886, when a man stood to his feet and said, " . . . I am going to trust, and I am going to obey."

Moody himself often said, *"The blood alone makes us safe; the Word alone makes us sure; but obedience alone makes us happy."* That was his formula for a successful Christian life and it is still a good one.

We need to trust the Creator to know what He is doing—to know the end from the beginning—and do things His way. We need to obey Him, for there truly is no other way to be happy once we are "in Jesus" but to trust and obey Him.

Because Adam and Eve disobeyed, Genesis 6:5-7 says the fruit of their bodies filled the earth with wickedness and evil. Yet Adam and Eve and their offspring were intended to fill the earth with the glory of God. All that was needed was for that first couple to walk in obedience to God. The consequence of obedience would be that the earth would be filled with the glory of God. But . . .

### Adam and Eve were not obedient

Those vessels that were meant to bring the glory of God to earth began to fill it with wickedness. You see, both obedience and disobedience multiply and produce fruit of their own kind on this earth. Adam and Eve disobeyed before they had produced *even one unfallen offspring* to be God's agent of redemption! All of the offspring they were able to produce thus arrived in this world already "fallen" and needing to be restored to a right relationship with the Creator.

Within seven generations from Adam, bodies that were made to fill the earth with God's glory had filled the earth wickedness and violence. With a little simple math, we can conclude that if Adam had been obedient to God, then in seven generations the mission God planned for the human body to accomplish would have been fulfilled. The earth, just like the heavens, would have by then been able to *"declare the glory of God."*[4]

If Adam and Eve had fulfilled their God-given destiny, the bodies that were made to house the glory of God would have so procreated in seven generations that the planet would have been filled with God's presence. There would be have been no place here for the enemy. But that's not how it happened.

## God did not give up on His creation

God kept alive His messianic promise to Eve[5] through Noah, the man who *"found grace in the eyes of the Lord . . . a just man . . . "* who *"walked with God."*[6] God destroyed every human being on the planet except those of the household of this one man who had been found faithful.

God's glory was almost totally removed from the earth. That was a significant development in the history of mankind. Periodically, over the course of human history, God did break through the overall hardness of human hearts and commune with those few who were faithful. Enoch, Noah, Abraham, Isaac, Jacob, Joseph, and Moses are recorded as having had personal encounters with the God of Israel. However, God's glory was generally removed from the earth when Adam and Eve disobeyed in the garden.

Their disobedience had a double consequence. Not only did it leave the *world outside the glory of God*; it left the world firmly *in the grip of Satan and evil*. It was not until Moses obeyed God and led the children of Israel in a sacrifice of spotless lambs that the continuing, visible evidence of God's presence returned to the human family. On that night after the celebration of the first Passover, when the children of Israel left the bondage of Egypt, God's presence in the cloud of smoke by day and pillar of fire by night came to lead them to the Promised Land. Joseph, whose bones they carried out of Egypt with them, had foretold the return of God's presence to earth by prophesying, *"God will surely visit you."* [7]

For the entire 40 years in the desert, they would follow the cloud by day and the fire by night. God never took His presence away from them, even though many of them at times turned away from Him. This was the first special revelation of God to the human family since the fall of Adam.

In the tabernacle, which Moses built in strict obedience to the pattern God revealed to him on Mount Sinai, God dwelt among Israel in the form of the cloud by day and the fire by night. However, He did not dwell within each human being. But eventually, disobedience cost Israel that marvelous manifestation of God's presence that hung visibly over their wandering nation. The cloud of smoke and pillar of fire disappeared.

Centuries later, God's continuing desire to dwell on earth would be manifested by the return of His glory to the Temple of Solomon. When the temple was dedicated in Jerusalem, the priests were unable to stand to minister because of the glory of God in the Ark of the Covenant.

### Disobedience separates us from God's presence

But once again, human disobedience resulted in the removal of God's glory from the earth. The Israelites blamed God for a setback in battle with the Philistines and moved the Ark of the Covenant from where He had told them to leave it, trusting in their wisdom rather than God's. Israel was soundly defeated and the Philistines captured the Ark. God's visible presence was again absent from Israel and from the earth.

The old priest Eli died from the shock of hearing about the Ark and the loss of his two sons in the battle. His daughter-in-law went into labor at the news that her husband was dead. She instructed that the baby boy born to her that day be named Ichabod, meaning, *"The glory has departed from Israel."*[8] "Ichabod" was eventually written over all Israel. The glory of the Lord departed.

In the tabernacle and the temple, God dwelled *among* men, not *in* them. Sin prevented Him from dwelling *in* men. Let's just let that thought settle in for a moment while we turn our attention to Christ's body and remind ourselves what the Holy Spirit says of Him in Hebrews 10:1-10 (NASB):

> *"For the Law, since it has only a shadow of the good things to come and not the very form of things, can never by the same sacrifices year by year, which they offer continually, make perfect those who draw near.*

> *"Otherwise, would they not have ceased to be offered, because the worshipers, having once been cleansed, would no longer have had consciousness of sins? But in those sacrifices there is a reminder of sins year by year. For it is impossible for the blood of bulls and goats to take away sins.*

> *"Therefore, when He comes into the world, He says: 'Sacrifice and offering Thou hast not desired, But a body Thou hast prepared for Me; In whole burnt offerings and sacrifices for sin Thou hast taken no pleasure.'*

*"Then I said, 'Behold, I have come (In the roll of the book it is written of Me) To do Thy will, O God.'"*

*"After saying above, 'Sacrifices and offerings and whole burnt offerings and sacrifices for sin Thou hast not desired, nor hast Thou taken pleasure in them' (which are offered according to the Law), then He said, 'Behold, I have come to do Thy will.' He takes away the first in order to establish the second.*

*"By this will we have been sanctified through the offering of the body of Jesus Christ once for all."*

### The Second Adam would not fail in His mission

In the womb of the virgin Mary, God prepared another earthen urn to house His presence. One thing about this urn that was different from the first urn made at creation was that, this time, God himself would dwell in the urn. *"And the Word became flesh, and dwelt among us, and we beheld His glory, glory as of the only begotten from the Father, full of grace and truth."*[9] And as Paul would remind us, in the body of Jesus there resided *"the fullness of the power of the Godhead bodily,"*[10] drawing attention to the fact that God still wants to dwell in a human body.

Unlike Adam's body, which so quickly became a *tragedy* in the chronicles of God's dealings with humanity, Christ's body would be the source of His *triumph* over sin. Through Him, we, too, are *"more than conquerors"*[11] over sin. The difference between *Adam and Christ* is the difference between *disobedience and obedience*.

Obedience was the law of Jesus' life. In the temple, when a very frightened Mary and Joseph questioned Him about His disappearance, he explained that He had a higher mission to fulfill: *"Wist ye not that I must be about my father's business?"*[12] In the Garden of Gethsemane, He agonized over the cup of human sin and conceded, *"My Father, if it is possible, let this cup pass from Me; yet not as I will, but as Thou wilt."*[13] Paul says, *"He humbled himself, and became obedient unto death, even the death of the cross."*[14]

Through His death and resurrection, He who *is* the glory of God regained access to that glory for the whole human family. Through His high priestly ministry of intercession for us, we may be sanctified by the offering of His body and His blood so that our bodies can become temples of His presence.

This leads me to a simple question: Is this body a tragedy or a triumph? Spiritually speaking, we prevail or we fall *in the body*. Paul says, in 1 Corinthians 9:27 (NASB), *"I keep under my body, and bring it into subjection: lest that by any means, when I have preached to others, I myself should become a castaway."*

In our primary text for this message, Jesus, at the Last Supper, reminds the twelve that His body and blood are about to be offered for their sins. He has tried to help them understand that He is that Bread of God sent down from heaven; the bread from which, if men eat, they shall never hunger or die. He's tried to help them understand that if they will deny themselves and obey Him, He will live in them, and they will never die. And yet, seated at the table among His twelve closest followers, there was one who would betray Him and one who would deny even knowing Him.

Jesus was able to predict Judas' betrayal and Peter's denial because He knew that neither of them had yet given their bodies to Him. Betrayal took place in Judas' heart long before he bargained with another person to betray the Lord. And denial took place in Peter's heart long before he opened his mouth to speak those words. Jesus knew what both men would do because He knew the condition of each man's heart and how that condition would be played out in each man's body.

I don't think I need to belabor the point that the body becomes a manifestation of the spiritual presence it houses. When we disobey God's Word, we resemble our fallen forebear, Adam. When we obey, we resemble our risen Lord. And the choice to disobey or obey is made hundreds of times each day as a result of the spiritual warfare that's fought over whose presence will be expressed in our bodies.

Peter recovered from his tragedy. Judas didn't. It's difficult to tell who will and who won't: the only predictor is what we decide to do about betraying or denying our Lord once we realize what we've done. Of course, the best way to deal with betraying or denying the Lord is to win that battle *in your mind* before your thoughts or intents become deeds, and never let it happen.

Here among us this morning are some wounded soldiers of the cross. If they felt secure enough to talk to us out of their hearts, they would tell us of battles poorly fought and lost. They would warn us that the same thoughts that went through their mind go through ours. They would try to help us recognize the danger signs and draw back from the brink of impending disaster before something similar happens to us. Although an ambulance at the bottom of the cliff is better than no protection at all, what we need most is a good fence at the top!

These brothers in the Lord haven't been any more careless than some of the rest of us have been, but they are the ones who have been exposed. If we could hear the cries of our brothers' hearts this morning, we would no longer be deceived into thinking that if our sins are hidden before men, they are hidden before God. His Word plainly says, *"Be not deceived; God is not mocked: for whatsoever a man [or a woman] soweth, that shall he [or she] also reap."*[15]

**We will all stand before the Judgment Seat of Christ**

The products of the body—its fruit—will one day be tried at the Judgment Seat of Christ. On that day God will call each of us individually into account for the stewardship of our body.

This is a natural part of the laws of the harvest. When you sow kernels of corn, you get a cornstalk with several ears of corn on it. *If we sow, we're going to reap. We're going to reap the same thing we sow. And we're going to reap more than we sow.*

The simple things we do in obedience to God often go unnoticed here on earth. But they do not go unnoticed by our heavenly Father. That's what the Judgment Seat of Christ is all about. There our Lord will reveal the eternal residual or wealth of our life on earth. From 1 Corinthians 3:15, we clearly see that that some believers will arrive in heaven with no eternal residual from their life on earth, *". . . saved; yet so as by fire."* On that day Jesus will reveal who each of us has allowed to live in his or her body.

Sometimes I think we forget that this battle we fight for the body is twofold; we are not only to refuse expression to evil, we are to express good. We have a theological word for the urge to do evil: we call it *temptation.* And we all want to be on guard to resist temptation. However, we have no theological word for the urge to do good. I like to think of the urge to do good as *divine opportunity.* I believe this is what Paul was referring to in Galatians 6:10, *"As we have therefore opportunity, let us do good unto all men, especially unto them who are of the household of faith."*

We need to be alert to those divine urges so that we can overcome evil with good. Of course we need to remain aware of the sound of the enemy's voice, too, urging us to behave in destructive ways. But we need even more to be acutely aware of and sensitive to the voice of the risen Lord who visits those with *"ears to hear,"*[16] bringing divine urges to do good.

### God wants to dwell in our earthen vessels

Being born again makes it possible for us to house the glory of God *in our bodies.* The same glory that was *above* the tabernacle in the wilderness and *above* the temple in Jerusalem can dwell *in* this earthen vessel. The glory of God is the treasure the human body was created to house. It gives forth an unmistakable radiance and light manifested in the good works we do for His kingdom. *"Let your light so shine before men, that they may see your good works, and glorify your Father which is in heaven."*[17] Hallelujah!

We are to exhibit less and less evil in our lives. We are to produce more and more good works—inspired by our heavenly Father—which bring glory to Him.

In 1 Corinthians 3:17 and 6:19,20 , we are reminded that the body is a *"temple."* And 2 Corinthians 5:1 (NASB) calls the body a *"tent."* What *is* a tent or a temple but a place to house something; or, more appropriately, some*one*? The question for us this morning, then, is, *For whom is my body—your body—a dwelling place? Who dwells there?*

The presence living and manifesting itself in our bodies is determined simply by our disobedience or obedience to God's written and Living Word. He wants us to house His glory in our earthen vessels. That's why He made them:

*"For God, who said, 'Light shall shine out of darkness,' is the One who has shone in our hearts to give the light of the knowledge of the glory of God in the face of Christ. But we have this treasure in earthen*

*vessels, that the surpassing greatness of the power may be of God and not from ourselves.*"[18]

Where has this treasure been placed? It has been given to us in our hearts, in the center of our being. And what is the treasure? It is the light of the knowledge of the glory of God in the face of Jesus Christ.

This is the *Shekinah glory* alluded to in the Old Testament, an expression literally translated as *the dwelling of God.* It is spoken of in Isaiah 60:2 (NASB): "*. . . the Lord will rise upon you, and His glory will appear upon you. And nations will come to your light.*" This is the same glory and presence of God that Moses wrote about in Exodus 13:21 and 14:19,20, in the cloud of smoke by day and the pillar of fire by night. This Shekinah is the treasure that is to inhabit our bodies. As we've already read, we have this "*. . . treasure in earthen vessels, that the surpassing greatness of the power may be of God and not from ourselves.*"

God not only wants us to *house* His glory in our earthen vessels; He wants that glory to *grow* in us. In 2 Corinthians 3:17,18, we read:

> "*Now the Lord is that Spirit: and where the Spirit of the Lord is, there is liberty. But we all, with open [unveiled] face beholding as in a glass the glory of the Lord, are changed into the same image from glory to glory, even as by the Spirit of the Lord.*"

This means that as we behold the Lord in His written and Living Word, a manifestation of His presence should be more and more obvious in our bodies, revealed as light in the darkness of this world through our attitudes and our deeds.

The older we get, the more visible is the tragedy or triumph of our bodies; the more obvious it becomes whose servant we are. There is no comparison between an aged servant of Satan and an aged saint of God. You can see in the harvest of a person's life and their countenance exactly who they have served and what that servitude has done to them or for them.

We're approaching the Lord's Table this morning. And today, as He does every time we observe this ordinance of the Church, He gives us the opportunity to examine ourselves. You need to ask yourself, and I need to ask myself this morning, "What is the source of the law by which I live my life? Am I being ruled by the selfish spirit of disobedience or by the self-sacrificing spirit of obedience to God?"

We are coming into the presence of One Whose eyes see deeper parts of us than are accessible to any human parent. He sees far more than any earthly mom or dad could ever see when they were trying to determine whether we were being honest with them. And it behooves us to pay attention to Him when He tells us what He sees in those deep parts of us.

If there is denial in us, may we not need—as Peter did—a little maid by a fire to reveal it to us.[19] If there is betrayal in us, may we not need to be publicly identified as a traitor in order to recognize it.[20] Instead, may we be willing to expose ourselves to the One Who can sanctify us with His blood; Who can turn our tragedy into His triumph; Who can spare us the harvest of a life of disobedience. May we be willing to open ourselves to the One Who can enable us through His grace to celebrate the fruits of obedience as each of us exposes our innermost being to Him today, privately and personally. And now, as we approach His Table, *"So let a man examine himself."*

Christ wants to dwell in you. He wants to dwell in me. And until His life is being expressed in your body and in mine, each of us is falling far short of the purpose for which our earthly body was created.

In a moment we're going to partake of the Bread which is part of the Communion observance and we'll hear His words, *"This is my body, which is broken for you."* As we eat that Bread and hear those words, my personal and heartfelt prayer is:

*Lord, help me not only to remember that this broken piece of bread is an emblem of Your body; help the hand that holds it remind me of my need to be sure my body is available to express Your glory. I want Your glory to be expressed in my body. I want Your presence to empower me to overcome my natural bent toward disobedience so that I can walk in obedience before You. I want to be aware that there is a growing glory of God coming from my earthen vessel and spilling out into our sin-darkened world.*

Shall we pray together.

*Father, as we bow before You today, in the Name of Jesus, may it be as though we were there in that Upper Room with the twelve. May we be aware that just as Your Son looked around upon them, He looks around upon us. Not only does He look upon us; He sees within us.*

*Whatever needs to be put in order, whatever tables need to be overturned, whatever uncleanness needs to be driven out, may we take advantage of these moments of self-examination to clean up our lives with Your help before we eat the bread and drink the cup. As we then eat the bread and drink the cup, may a fresh infusion of Your glory come to each of us, reminding us that our bodies have been created to house Your presence. In Jesus' Name we pray, Amen.*

(Congregational singing: "Take My Life and Let It Be," and "My Jesus, I Love Thee.")

Now let's look to God for His blessing upon the bread.

*Lord Jesus, we hold in our hands an emblem of Your broken body. We understand that through Your obedience, those of us who by nature are disobedient can be cleansed and sanctified, given grace to obey, and have the thrill of knowing that in us is One who is greater than "he that is in the world."*

*Those among us who are ill and afflicted are looking to You for healing this morning, but we also want to look beyond the gift of healing to its purpose. For, among the reasons why You heal us is so that our bodies might be made whole in order to give full expression to the Lord Who dwells within.*

*And so we ask, Lord, that You touch and heal those who need it; not just for our convenience, but that our bodies might be more fit to express the presence of the One Who lives within us. Our bodies truly are temples of Your Holy Spirit. As we partake of the bread this morning, remind us of that. Quicken our bodies; touch us and heal us so that we might give full energy to the expression of Christ's life within us. In His Name we pray, Amen.*

*" . . . The Lord Jesus the same night in which he was betrayed took bread: And when he had given thanks, he brake it, and said, Take,*

*eat: this is my body, which is broken for you: this do in remembrance of me.* "[21]

Shall we eat together.

*(Inspirational prophetic word: For God has not chosen to live in idols made of wood or stone or metal, but God has chosen to live in vessels of clay, urns He fashioned from the earth to house His presence. He longs to dwell within you. He longs to dwell within you. He longs to sup with you. He longs to walk with you. He longs to live and express himself in you and through you. So, open the gates of the temple, and let the King of glory come in. For as you dedicate yourself to His presence, He will come and fill you with His glory. Hallelujah! And the glory of the Lord shall shine forth upon you. And all the world shall know that He dwells not only among you but He lives within you.)*

*Hallelujah be to God! Hallelujah be to God! Come in, Lord Jesus. Burst forth in new dimensions within us, we pray. Hallelujah!*

And now let's ask His blessing on the cup.

*We hold in our hands, Lord Jesus, an emblem so sacred we don't even know how to properly receive it. Oh, God, help us never to take the emblems of Your body and blood for granted. May we never lose our sense of awe and wonder at what they represent.*

*Oh, God, as we partake of this cup today, let each of us examine ourselves. Let each of us confess our sins to You. Let each of us present ourselves to be freshly cleansed and sanctified so that, as we partake of this cup, every weight might be laid aside and every besetting sin might be cast off.*

*And in this moment, Lord, may we celebrate purity; may we celebrate cleanness; may we celebrate sanctity and holiness; even as we've been admonished, Lord, in this meeting. May our bodies be rededicated. May our souls be cleansed afresh and made ready to receive from You a greater dimension of the presence of Christ, our Lord. In Jesus' Name we pray, Amen.*

*"And he took the cup, and gave thanks, and gave it to them, saying, Drink ye all of it; For this is my blood of the new testament, which is shed for many for the remission of sins."* [22]

Shall we drink together.

And now let's sing together in closing our Communion service: "See His Glory Come Down."

---

[1] Luke 22:14-22, NASB.
[2] Genesis 1:26.
[3] Psalm 8:3-6, NASB.
[4] Psalm 19:1.
[5] Genesis 3:15.
[6] Genesis 6:8,9.
[7] Exodus 13:18-22.
[8] 1 Samuel 4:21.
[9] John 1:14, NASB
[10] Colossians 2:9.
[11] Romans 8:37.
[12] Luke 2:41-49.
[13] Matthew 26:39, NASB.
[14] Philippians 2:8.
[15] Galatians 6:7.
[16] Luke 8:8.
[17] Matthew 5:16.
[18] 2 Corinthians 4:6,7, NASB.
[19] Mark 14:66-68.
[20] Matthew 26:47-50.
[21] 1 Corinthians 11:23,24.
[22] Matthew 26:27,28.

# 11
## Feed the Fire *

The architecture of our church speaks to the priorities of our theology. While we have modernized the pulpit and brought it closer to both the floor level of the building and the congregational seating area, it still occupies a place of central importance in the sanctuary. The purpose of a pulpit is to remind us that the Word of God stands on its own—it needs no man or woman to support it. God's Word is its own proof; either we believe it or we don't. And it is central to who we are and what we are about. I do not stand behind this desk to draw attention to myself. I stand behind this desk this morning to bring God's Word to His people because that is the task to which He called me today.

Bridging the gap between us—as the people of God—and the holy requirements of God's Word stands the Communion Table. This Table and the emblems it holds are a reminder that Jesus' life, death, and resurrection satisfied the demands of a holy God for human beings to be saved from a life of sin and enter into an eternal relationship with God through His Son. [1]

Well, let's get into our message. When Jesus was not preaching or teaching, He loved to be with people. He loved to sit *"at meat"* with *"publicans and sinners."* [2] It bothers me that as ministers of the gospel we are uncomfortable with sinners; that we don't like to go to social events where sinners will be present. Salt is no good in a box and light is of no benefit where the sun already shines. We need to be where the rot is. That's where salt is of the greatest benefit. We need to be where

---

* Sermon for the Communion Service of the 1995 Ohio District Council of the Assemblies of God, Dayspring Assembly of God, Bowling Green, Ohio.

darkness is at its worst, because that's where the light shines at its brightest.

We Pentecostal preachers need to do more than just bring a charismatic presence to the pulpit and deliver the message God puts on our heart. We need to put some shoe leather under those sermons and take them out into the streets where the sinners live and eat and work. We need to spend some of our time sitting *"at meat"* with those who still don't know there's a God Who loves them and can show them a better way to live. And that brings me to our Scripture reading for this morning.

> *"Now that same day two of them were going to a village called Emmaus, about seven miles from Jerusalem. They were talking with each other about everything that had happened. As they talked and discussed these things with each other, Jesus himself came up and walked along with them; but they were kept from recognizing him. He asked them, 'What are you discussing together as you walk along?'*
>
> *"They stood still, their faces downcast. One of them, named Cleopas, asked him, 'Are you only a visitor to Jerusalem and do not know the things that have happened there in these days?'*
>
> *"'What things?' he asked.*
>
> *"'About Jesus of Nazareth,' they replied. 'He was a prophet, powerful in word and deed before God and all the people. The chief priests and our rulers handed him over to be sentenced to death, and they crucified him; but we had hoped that he was the one who was going to redeem Israel. And what is more, it is the third day since all this took place. In addition, some of our women amazed us. They went to the tomb early this morning but didn't find his body. They came and told us that they had seen a vision of angels, who said he was alive. Then some of our companions went to the tomb and found it just as the women had said, but him they did not see.'*
>
> *"He said to them, 'How foolish you are, and how slow of heart to believe all that the prophets have spoken! Did not the Christ have to suffer these things and then enter his glory?' And*

*beginning with Moses and all the Prophets, he explained to them what was said in all the Scriptures concerning himself.*

*"As they approached the village to which they were going, Jesus acted as if he were going farther. But they urged him strongly, 'Stay with us, for it is nearly evening: the day is almost over.' So he went in to stay with them.*

*"When he was at the table with them, he took bread, gave thanks, broke it and began to give it to them. Then their eyes were opened and they recognized him, and he disappeared from their sight. They asked each other, 'Were not our hearts burning within us while he talked with us on the road and opened the Scriptures to us?'*

*"They got up and returned at once to Jerusalem. There they found the Eleven and those with them, assembled together and saying, 'It is true! The Lord has risen and has appeared to Simon.' Then the two told what had happened on the way, and how Jesus was recognized by them when he broke the bread.*

*"While they were still talking about this, Jesus himself stood among them and said to them, 'Peace be with you.' They were startled and frightened, thinking they saw a ghost. He said to them, 'Why are you troubled, and why do doubts rise in your minds? Look at my hands and my feet. It is I myself! Touch me and see: a ghost does not have flesh and bones, as you see I have.'*

*"When he had said this, he showed them his hands and feet. And while they still did not believe it because of joy and amazement, he asked them, 'Do you have anything here to eat?' They gave him a piece of broiled fish, and he took it and ate it in their presence.*

*"He said to them, 'This is what I told you while I was still with you: Everything must be fulfilled that is written about me in the Law of Moses, the Prophets, and the Psalms.'*

*"Then he opened their minds so they could understand the Scriptures. He told them, 'This is what is written: The Christ will suffer and rise from the dead on the third day, and repentance*

*and forgiveness of sins will be preached in his name to all nations, beginning at Jerusalem. You are witnesses of these things. I am going to send you what my Father has promised; but stay in the city until you have been clothed with power from on high.'* "[3]

I want to focus on part of verse 32, *"Were not our hearts burning within us?"* And I want to couple that with 1 Thessalonians 5:19 (NIV): *"Do not put out the Spirit's fire."*

Shall we pray.

*Father, I want to thank You this morning for meeting us in this 50th District Council; for all the prayers that have gone up for this meeting. For the intense hunger that was expressed following our Superintendent's challenging message last night. For that same kind of hunger that was obvious this morning as we gathered for prayer.*

*Lord, let this be the beginning of a surge of hunger in us for more of You. Help us feed the fire of every tiny flame You kindle in our hearts. And as we gather this morning at Your table, reveal Yourself to us as You did to the two on the way to Emmaus. Let us leave this morning's service with burning hearts, determined that we will not put out the fire of the Spirit. In Jesus' Name we pray, Amen.*

Today, Pentecostals comprise the fastest-growing Christian movement on earth. No less a skeptic than the Harvard theologian Harvey Cox, in his book, **Fire from Heaven**, acknowledges that we are growing faster than the militant Islam and Christian fundamentalists. In Africa, Pentecostal congregations are rapidly becoming the main expression of Christianity. In several Latin American countries, there are Pentecostal majorities where Roman Catholicism once dominated.

Pentecostals now comprise a movement estimated at over 400 million people. What is the secret of this phenomenal growth? How do we account for it? The secret, as we all know, is found in the testimony of these two disciples on the road to Emmaus: *"Were not our hearts burning within us while he talked with us on the road and opened the Scriptures to us?"* Like these two disciples, Pentecostals historically have been people who walked daily with the resurrected Christ and whose hearts were set on fire by Him.

Paul was anticipating that believers would tend to leave their first love when he admonished the Thessalonians (1 Thessalonians 5:19), *"Do not put out the Spirit's fire."* It concerns many of us that while Pentecostal fires burn brightly on other continents and in other countries, barely 50 percent of the people who attend Assemblies of God churches in this country regularly speak in other tongues. I believe God will always have people whose hearts are on fire for Him, for He faithfully sends the fire. *My concern is that we stay a part of those people.* And if the fire is to remain, each of us must take the responsibility of feeding the fire He sends into our hearts and our lives.

### What *is* the Pentecostal fire?

You cannot gain an accurate estimate of the temperature that blazes in anyone's heart from behavior in a joint worship service. You *walk in the Spirit* where you live and where you work. The early Pentecostal movement found its secret of growth in the power to translate those tremendously inspirational services into practical, daily expressions in the workplace, the marketplace, and the neighborhood. They not only *fed* the fire . . . *they took it with them everywhere they went.*

We might ask ourselves this simple question, What is this fire? What does it mean to have our hearts "burn" within us? What is the "fire" of Pentecost?

In the Old Testament, fire was the symbol of God's presence. In fact, throughout the Scriptures, God announces His presence by fire. In Genesis 15:17,18, God seals His covenant with Abraham by fire. In Exodus 3:2, He calls Moses from a bush that's on fire. In Exodus 13:22, He promises to guide Israel through every night by a pillar of fire. In Exodus 19:18, He confirms His covenant with Israel by fire. In Leviticus 6:12, He commands that the fire on the brazen altar never go out.

In 1 Kings 18:38, He honors Elijah's challenge to the prophets of Baal and proves himself as the God who answers by fire. In 2 Kings 2:11, He takes Elijah to heaven in a chariot of fire. In Isaiah 6:6,7, it was a coal of fire from heaven's altar that touched the prophet's tongue.

In Matthew 3:11, John the Baptist says Jesus is the one who will *"baptize you with the Holy Ghost and with fire."* In Acts 2:3,4 Luke records that the room was filled with, *"Cloven tongues like as of fire, and it sat upon each of them. And they were all filled with the Holy Ghost, and began to speak with other tongues, as the Spirit gave them utterance.*" In Revelation 19:12, Jesus is the rider of the white horse whose eyes are *"as a flame of fire,"* and (in v. 16) the one on whose thigh is written the name, *"KING OF KINGS, AND LORD OF LORDS."*

Numbers 16:35 and 2 Chronicles 7:1 are among the Scriptures that remind us our God is a *consuming* kind of fire. The closer we get to Him, the more our hearts become ablaze with the glory of His presence. That's what the *fire* is all about.

### What is the purpose of the Pentecostal fire?

The fire of God's presence in my heart and yours is first of all to kindle a passionate love for God. Jesus says this is the first commandment: *"Thou shalt love the Lord thy God with all thy heart, and with all thy soul, and with all thy mind."*[4] Once God kindles that fire, the secret to a heart that *stays* on fire is feeding the hunger the Holy Spirit gives us for God: *"Blessed are they which do hunger and thirst after righteousness: for they shall be filled."*[5]

This holy fire that passionately consumes us in a love for God should also be expressed in a passionate love for our spouse (if we are married) and for our family. It doesn't make much sense to a wife, a husband, or a child to have a spouse or parent who claims to be on fire for God *unless that fire is translated in terms of tender love* for wife and parental love for children.

We also need to treat our brothers and sisters in Christ lovingly. One of the things that concerns me—and I hope concerns many of us— is that we don't always show our love for each other in the body of Christ. We tend to be more critical than compassionate toward Christian brothers and sisters. This is why Sunday morning worship services have become more pretentious than real. People don't come to church on Sunday morning to be honest about the sins of the past week. Why? They are afraid of the criticism of their brothers and sisters in the Body of Christ.

It's harder to be honest about your sins in church than in any other place you go. We don't love each other enough to to be honest about spiritual shortcomings in front of each other. Jesus did *not* say, "By this shall all men know that ye are my disciples, that your doctrine is without error." He didn't say, "By this shall all men know that ye are my disciples, that your life is without error." He said, *"By this shall all men know that ye are my disciples, if ye love one to another."* [6] And let's not forget, *"Beloved, let us love one another: for love is of God . . . He that loveth not knoweth not God; for God is love."*[7]

The love we have for our spouse; the love we have for our child; the love we have for our brother and sister in Christ; that love should also spill out onto our neighbor. We need to ask ourselves, "If I was the only Christian this person ever talked to, would they see the difference Jesus can make in someone's life when the going gets rough? Would they be able to see the joy in serving Him whether times are good or bad? Do they see love and concern in the way I treat them?"

### Loving others into the kingdom of God

This is how the early church grew—by loving people into the kingdom of God. They didn't have seminars on church growth. Instead, *" . . . continuing daily with one accord in the temple, and breaking bread from house to house, [they] did eat their meat with gladness and singleness of heart, Praising God, and having favour with all the people. And the Lord added to the church daily such as should be saved."*[8]

The Holy Ghost fire we're talking about must break through in our neighborliness. We must somehow communicate to our people and model for them a neighborliness that entertains people other than close family in our homes through the year. Amen?!

We've lost contact with the unbelievers in our world. And *transfer growth* has been revealed to most of us for what it really represents: *stagnation*. A Methodist brother went to his pastor and said to him, "Do you think it would matter much if I went to the Baptist church?"

The Methodist pastor reflected for a moment and said, "No, I don't think it hurts much to change the label on an empty bottle." Some people call this "playing musical churches." That's what we're talking about when we speak of *transfer growth*. We don't need endless transfer growth. We need *evangelism growth*. And we can't win a world to a Christ until our hearts are so much on fire with His love that we realize our *house* is too little for *God's Lamb*. Do you remember the story of the lamb of the

Passover? In instructing Israel how they should celebrate the Passover, God told them, *" . . . each man is to take a lamb for his family, one for each household. If any household is too small for a whole lamb, they must share one with their nearest neighbor."*[9] Our house is too little for God's Lamb. We must not selfishly consume Him ourselves; we must share Christ with our neighbors.

### Protect your heart from becoming hardened

There is but a short distance between our loss of concern for others and the hardening of our hearts toward God. When we lose the fire of God in our hearts, we begin to lose our concern for others. Our hearts become hard, even toward those we love.

In Matthew 19:8, Jesus identifies *hardening of the heart* as the central cause of divorce. I never thought I'd see the day when the church would need a ministry to children of divorce—*who belong to Christian parents*. But that day is here. And the reason there is divorce among Christians is because hearts are cold and hard. We do not feed the fire . . . we do not stay warm and tender before God or warm and tender toward each other. Paul admonishes us, *"And be ye kind one to another, tenderhearted, forgiving one another, even as God for Christ's sake hath forgiven you."*[10]

The root cause of many mental health problems is in our stubborn refusal to forgive those who trespass against us. In similar fashion, at the heart of many spiritually cold churches are bygone congregational issues that have never been addressed and forgiven. The way to keep our churches from becoming spiritually cold is to appropriate the fire of God, when it begins to fall, to empower us to confess our faults one to another and pray one for another that God will heal us.

Many of us can remember times when we had genuine *Holy Ghost revivals*. We know that a *Holy Ghost revival* is always accompanied by the breaking of Christians' hearts with the love of God. It's accompanied by the confessing of our faults to one another; by love that flows among us from the Holy Spirit's refining flame, enabling us to put past issues behind us. In Psalm 51:17, David reminds us through the words of his prayer, *" . . . a broken and a contrite heart, O God, thou wilt not despise."* When you find a heart that's on fire, you find a heart that's broken and a spirit that's contrite.

The fire of God's presence is to enlighten us. God's Word is to be a *"lamp unto my feet.*"[11] I want to express right here a concern I have for our Assemblies of God worship services today. There have always been times when God has moved in tremendous ways in our services before the preaching of the Word. We have enjoyed and benefited tremendously from this unique blessing. But the *novelty* of those times that occurred with some regularity a few years ago has become *accepted tradition*. It seems as if our emphasis has changed. I personally am concerned that the emphasis and highlight of many Assemblies of God and other Pentecostal services today seems to be on the worship time, not following the preaching of God's Word.

Friends, Jesus did not say that salvation and changed lives and the fire of God in a person's life would follow *worship times*. He said miraculous signs would follow the preaching of the Word: *"Go ye into all the world, and preach the gospel to every creature. He that believeth and is baptized shall be saved; but he that believeth not shall be damned. And these signs shall follow them that believe . . . ."*[12] We need to see results *following the preaching of the Word of God*.

Our Superintendent was so anointed of God last night, and said so many wonderful things along this line. I hesitate to try to add anything to what he said so well. But let me just add this one little postscript to his letter: Unless a practice can be supported by Scripture, it should never be normative in our fellowship. That which is novel comes and goes . . . but if it can't stand the test of Scripture, it has no permanent place in a Pentecostal church.

### The refining fire of God

The presence of God's fire is also to refine us. Peter admonishes us, *"That the trial of your faith, being much more precious than of gold that perisheth, though it be tried with fire, might be found unto praise and honor and glory at the appearing of Jesus Christ."*[13]

I wonder where we would be if we all got everything we ask God for. It's the things I don't welcome into my life that the Holy Spirit often uses to refine my faith. You don't find your faith refined on the mountaintop. Your faith is refined in the valley. You don't find your faith refined when God's blessing is pouring into your life. You find your faith refined when you pass through the fire. Sometimes we come through trials with a spouse's illnesses. I think nothing has refined me more than the loss of my first wife. We're refined through the rebellion of our children. If you think you can get from *your child's birth* to *your death* without experiencing any pain in the relationship with that child, you're a dreamer! Sometimes the pain comes sooner. Sometimes the pain comes later. But just as sure as it causes pain to get a child into this world, before *you* leave this world, you will go through some intense pain with your child.

*"Beloved, think it not strange concerning the fiery trial which is to try you, as though some strange thing happened unto you."*[14] Trial by fire is normal; it's the purification process by which the baggage that attaches itself to us over time is burned away.

As pastors, we not only go through the fire ourselves; we take the people of our congregation right through the flames with us when we are being purified. I've no doubt that people in our churches feel at times that they are "afflicted," rather than "blessed," with their pastor. Staff members go through the fire with senior pastors. Senior pastors go through the fire with staff members and deacons. But it's in those tough times in our relationships with other people that God burns the dross out of our lives and makes us wiser leaders. And our faith becomes more and more valuable to us because we find that it gets us through the fire.

### Trial by fire: the ultimate test of our earthly works

In 1 Corinthians 3:13, Paul reminds us that a trial by fire will be the ultimate test for each man's work; each woman's work: *"Every man's work shall be made manifest: for the day shall declare it, because it shall be revealed by fire; and the fire shall try every man's work of what sort it is."* If we come to the Lord's Table with the proper intent, we judge ourselves every time.

And when we come to this Table, we must also remind ourselves of the ultimate judgment—when we stand in His presence. Of course, we will never be judged for *our past sins* because Christ's sacrificial death on Calvary forever satisfied God's holy nature regarding our sins. However, *our works* will be judged. We need to make every visit to the Lord's Table a reminder of that coming judgment day and examine ourselves and our works in that light.

*I firmly believe that it's possible to save your soul and lose your life*. Let me explain. There will be people in heaven who were saved from hell by Christ's sacrifice for their sins, but at the same time they are people from whose earthly life Christ obtained no eternal benefit. When the revealing fire of God's judgment tries their works, and the wood, hay, and stubble flare up and are burned away, their 30, 50, 70, or 90 years on earth will all vanish. They'll still have their salvation. But the life He died to save will have brought Him no eternal glory.

God is not just interested in saving your soul; He wants your body, too. Remember, the purpose of the body is to manifest the presence of God on earth. And the only gold, silver, and precious stones that will be found in the works of my life or your life—when God tries them by fire as we stand in His presence—will be those things we did in His name, on His behalf.

### The any-time, any-place healing power of God

In the days of Jesus and the apostles, few healings and miracles took place in synagogues or churches. And there was good reason for this. Right or wrong, the healings and miracles that take place in large gatherings tend to be credited to the platform personality. And we are victimized, again and again, by this kind of idolization of our Pentecostal heroes.

Of course Jesus performed some very public miracles. He healed a man at the pool of Bethesda, in front of the large crowd who had gathered there to seek healing for themselves or a friend. He provided food for thousands of people from the remnants of a boy's sack lunch.

But a number of His miracles took place in smaller, more private settings. His first recorded miracle was performed *at a wedding feast* in Cana, in the highland country of Galilee. Another one took place *by Jacob's well* just outside the little Samarian village of Sychar, when He ministered to the needs of the Samaritan woman. He performed a miracle *in the home of a tax collector* in Jericho. He *interrupted a funeral procession* outside the village of Nain on a Galilee hillside in order to bring a young man back to life so that he might care for his widowed mother. When He raised Jairus' 12-year-old daughter from death, *there was no one in the room* except the girl, her parents, Jesus, Peter, James, and John. He performed the vast majority of His recorded miracles where the people—saints and sinners alike—lived and worked and carried on the business of their private lives.

Preachers can't take the Pentecostal fire everywhere. But the people of our churches can! They can spread it throughout the whole community through the refining fire of God which can clean away the dross and make them *so transparent that other that people can see Jesus* in the way they go about their daily lives.

### The Pentecostal experience is unique

Pentecostal revival fire is God's unique way of reaching the lost in these last days. And for some Pentecostal believers, that creates a unique dilemma. In recent decades, American Pentecostals have moved up in the world. Many among our number have gone from the "cottage" to the "mansion" *in this life*. Don't misunderstand me; there's nothing wrong with enjoying some of the fruit of your labor in the sweet now-and-now. But along the way, some of our brothers and sisters have become embarrassed and ashamed of their Pentecostal heritage. It doesn't fit their dignified new image or gain them the respect of those in the church world who have always looked down their noses at Pentecostals.

The Fundamentalist church world has never cared for Pentecostals. Evangelicals can swallow us, but we give them a stomach ache. And the Charismatics, who believe that you can be filled with the Holy Ghost today and not speak in tongues until a week or six months from now, tolerate us a little better—but they're not really sure about us, either. However, that kind of earthly approval really shouldn't matter. The loss of our Pentecostal fire is too great a price to pay in order to gain anyone's respect.

God laid His hand upon us as a unique people. Scripture clearly says that on a particular day, in a particular place, at a particular time, the first group of believers to experience this Baptism of the Holy Spirit " . . . *were all filled with the Holy Ghost, and began to speak with other tongues, as the Spirit gave them utterance.* "[15] It doesn't say the tongues-speaking came days or weeks or months later. It says they were *"filled"* and *"began to speak."* This Holy Ghost Baptism opens the door into the whole world of spiritual gifts; the supernatural and everything Pentecost has stood for. We dare not abandon it to gain the approval of others in the community!

We are *Pentecostal*. Being Pentecostal means we are talk in tongues. May we never deny it or be embarrassed by it. May we welcome it as an opening of the door into the *miracles and signs* ministry the Holy Spirit wants to accompany the preaching of the gospel.

The Evangelicals and the mainline churches, with all their missionary efforts, have not made the kind of impact the Pentecostals have made in Asia, Africa, South America, and the island nations of the earth. Why? Because no signs are following the preaching of the gospel.

Being Pentecostal does not make us holier than anyone else. Speaking in tongues has little to do with holiness of life. Being Pentecostal commits us to continuing in the 20th century the *miracles and signs* kind of ministry the Holy Spirit initiated in the Early Church as recorded in the Book of Acts. We are by tradition a people of burning hearts. May God help us feed that fire.

The kind of fire that heats your home has to be fed. The kind of fire that cooks your food has to be fed. The kind of fire that lights your path has to be fed. The kind of fire that empowers you to change the world for Christ also has to be fed. We must either feed the divine fire or lose it. And it's not enough to feed that fire twice a week when you come to church. We must *keep on keeping on* being filled with the Spirit: *"Speaking to yourselves in psalms and hymns and spiritual songs, singing and making melody in your hearts to the Lord."* [16] The only kind of fire that does not have to be fed is wildfire. Healthy fire *has to be fed*.

**How do we feed the fire?**

Our hearts need what the disciples had, if we are to stay on fire for our Lord. So . . . what exactly did they have?

First of all, they had a daily experience with Jesus. Being a disciple meant they quite literally followed Him: they went with Him wherever He went. They believed what He taught them and were committed to spreading His teachings to all who would listen. It was for this purpose that He first appeared to Peter and Cleopas and joined them on their journey to Emmaus. It almost goes without saying that Jesus wants to join me . . . Jesus wants to join you . . . on our journey through life, wherever we are. He wants to make disciples of us so that we can help make His presence known in our world.

It's easy to go ahead with life after you've been in the presence of Jesus and not realize you aren't beside Him any longer. The enemy sees to that. Even Jesus' parents had been away from Him for three days after they left the temple in Jerusalem before they realized He wasn't with them. The routine of life almost takes care of itself and you can go along for a long time without realizing what you've done, if you're not careful.

**You've got to feed the fire every day to keep it burning**

And you've heard me say it so many times you're probably tired of hearing it—but, one more time, let me say that I fear the professionalization of the ministry in our fellowship. Even the ministry is a job you can learn to excel in without the anointing of God. You don't have to have His anointing to preach well. Preaching is a skill that can be learned just like any of the performing arts. You can become very skilled at delivering these performances. And when you don't stay in close daily contact with Jesus, you won't even realize how the enemy wants to blind you to what you're doing. If even the parents of Jesus could go three days and not be aware He wasn't with them, how much easier prey we are! We have to be sure He's our daily companion. You can't have a hit-and-miss Christian walk and stay on fire. Daily contact is how we feed the fire.

One of the things I always think about when I'm preparing a message is whether there's anything I can do to help make it remain with people after the sound of my voice has died out of the auditorium. I have been particularly concerned about that with this message, and I've talked to Priscilla about it, because we both know how important it is to make sure Jesus is a part of our journey every day. Each of us can count on the enemy to try to drown the fire right out of our lives. And the Holy Spirit is too much of a gentleman to force His way into our lives. So, we were talking about whether there was anything we should do to keep this message alive for awhile in people's hearts.

And Priscilla said, "Well, honey, maybe we could just cut up some thin dowel rods . . . since sticks are one of the ways you feed a fire . . . maybe we could hand out little pieces of dowel rods at the end of the message. Men could carry them in the pocket where they keep their change. Women could put them in their change purse or wallet. And every time anybody was rummaging around for change, they would stumble over that little stick and it would remind them, *Did I feed the fire today?*

You see, it's not a matter of *getting* on fire . . . any revival can do that for you. It's a matter of *staying* on fire and realizing where the fire *comes from*: It's in *Jesus*. It's as *He* is revealed to us that our hearts begin burning within us. And like the manna in the wilderness, the touch of Jesus on our lives must be renewed each day. You can't go through today on yesterday's touch. Today's fire is not adequate to keep you warm tomorrow.

The apostles not only had an experience with Jesus; not only did the Living Word burn within them; Jesus exposed them to the written Word. An experience with the Living Word and exposure to the written Word—every day—is what is necessary to feed the fire.

Our experience with the Living Word is guided through our understanding of the written Word. And as the apostles discovered, when you're walking with the Living Word, He can make the written Word burn like fire in your bones.

**Open your heart to the fire of God**

The apostles did not recognize Jesus right away. They did not realize how cold their hearts had become in just a matter of days . . . until He shared a meal and *broke bread* with them. This was not a Communion service. No cup was shared. Jesus had said at the Last Supper that He would not drink from the cup or eat the bread of the Communion observance until that day when we celebrate it with Him in the kingdom of God. However, when Jesus broke bread with them, it apparently reminded them of the Last Supper He had shared with them. Something about the custom of breaking open the loaf of bread . . . something about the way He did it . . . opened their spiritual eyes and they realized the flame had again touched their hearts. *"Did not our hearts [then] burn within us?"*

As we celebrate the Lord's Supper, may He who joined the disciples on the road to Emmaus walk among us as the One who walked among the candlesticks.[17] As we break bread together today, may He open our eyes and reveal His risen glory to us. For it's only when He is lifted up that the whole world is drawn unto Him: *"And I, if I be lifted up from the earth, will draw all men unto me.* "[18] May the flame of His presence set our hearts afire, and may we be determined to feed that fire daily. The little piece of wood you're about to receive—put it somewhere and let it remind you, "Have I fed the fire today?"

### Are you on fire or burned out?

If you feed the fire, it's not likely to go out and you're not likely to burn out. There's a big difference between being *on fire* in the ministry and being *burned out* in the ministry. The third verse of an old Pentecostal hymn, "I Will Praise Him," used to find us singing about being on fire:

> *"Then God's fire upon the altar Of my heart was set aflame;*
> *I shall never cease to praise Him, Glory, glory to His name!*
> *I will praise Him! I will praise Him! Praise the Lamb for sinners slain;*
> *Give Him glory, all ye people, For His blood can wash away each stain."*[19]

May the burning Lamb touch our lives today as we examine our hearts in His presence.

(Pause for congregational prayer time, quietly, in unison.)

While our hearts are open to the Lord and we're singing that song again, I'm going to ask the ushers to distribute those little pieces of wood to act as daily reminders for us. Let's sing the rest of that song together.

Just before the men distribute the Communion emblems to us this morning, I want to read 1 Corinthians 11:27-31 (NIV):

> *"Therefore, whoever eats the bread or drinks the cup of the Lord in an unworthy manner will be guilty of sinning against the body and blood of the Lord. A man ought to examine himself before he eats of the bread and drinks of the cup. For anyone who eats and drinks without recognizing the body of the Lord eats and drinks judgment on himself. That is why many among you are weak and sick, and a number of you have fallen asleep. But if we judged ourselves, we would not come under judgment. When we are judged by the Lord, we are being disciplined so that we will not be condemned with the world."*

And now as the emblems are being distributed, let's bring ourselves to judgment. Let's allow the flame of the Lamb to touch our lives again and worship the Lord together as we are ministered to in song.

(Solo: "It Is Well With My Soul.")

Let's just worship the Lord together.

(Congregational singing: "I Will Praise Him;" "I Surrender All.")

*Jesus, come alongside us. Join our journey where we are, Lord. If we're basking in success, humble us. If we're burdened and in the valley, lift us and encourage us, Lord. Praise you, Jesus.*

> *"The Lord Jesus the same night in which he was betrayed took bread: And when he had given thanks, he brake it, and said, Take, eat: this is my body, which is broken for you: this do in remembrance of me."* Shall we eat together.

*Let healing flow, Lord. Let grace flow, Lord. Let strength and encouragement flow today among us, Lord. Teach us how to edify one another, how to build up one another. Touch us with the passion of your heart today, Jesus. As we have brought ourselves in judgment, help us to pray with David,* "Search me, O God, and know my heart: try me, and know my thoughts: And see if there be any wicked way in me, and lead me in the way everlasting."[21]

*When we drink this cup, Lord, may it indeed be to us something more than a bit of juice or a moment in a religious ritual. May it be a fresh reminder of the cleansing of Your precious Blood. Make it as new and fresh as this moment, Lord.* "Though [our] sins be as scarlet, [let them become] as white as snow; though they be red like crimson, [let them] be as wool."[22] Let us hear the word of grace in our ears. "[You have] not dealt with us after our sins; nor rewarded us according to our iniquities . . . [But] As far as the east is from the west, so far [have you] removed our transgressions from us."[23] *Hallelujah be to God!*

*As the Holy Spirit helps us to be faithful in confessing our sins, Lord, help us to realize you are* "faithful and just to forgive us our sins, and to cleanse us from all unrighteousness,"[24] *so that we can* "walk in the light, as He is in the light . . . and the blood of Jesus Christ [can cleanse] us from all sin."[25]

*"After the same manner also he took the cup, when he had supped, saying, This cup is the new testament in my blood: this do ye, as oft as ye drink it, in remembrance of me."*[26] *"Drink ye all of it."*[27] Shall we drink together.

(Congregational praise and worship time.)

"Oh, the blood of Jesus; Oh, the blood of Jesus;
Oh, the blood of Jesus; It washes white as snow.
Hallelujah, hallelujah; hallelujah for the cross.
Hallelujah, hallelujah; it shall never suffer loss."

"When I Survey the Wondrous Cross"[28]

"To God Be the Glory"[29]

"All That Thrills My Soul is Jesus"[30]

(A message of prophecy: "For the Lord your God is able to save. For the Lord your God is able to deliver. Out of His presence He is calling . . . to bring to Him your broken heart, to bring to Him your defeat, and lay them at His feet for He will bring victory and He will raise to life your heart and your life, your soul and your ministry. For the Lord your God has called you today, to save you, to deliver you, to give you life again, and to renew and revive you. Let Him pour His strength and His life into you once again and renew your heart and soul, in the Name of Jesus.")

"I will serve Him because I love Him; He has given life to me.
I was nothing 'til Jesus found me; You have given life to me.
Heartaches; broken pieces; shattered dreams are why You died on
   Calvary.
Your touch is what I long for; You have given life to me.
Heartaches; broken pieces; wounded lives are why You died on
   Calvary.
Your touch is what I long for; You have given life to me."

---

[1] Dobbins, Richard D. **The Family-Friendly Church**. Creation House/ Strang Communications: Altamonte Springs, Florida, 1989.
[2] Matthew 9:10.

[3] Luke 24:13-48, NIV.

[4] Matthew 22:37.

[5] Matthew 5:6.

[6] John 13:35.

[7] 1 John 4:7,8.

[8] Acts 2:46,47.

[9] Exodus 12:3,4, NIV.

[10] Ephesians 4:32.

[11] Psalm 119:105.

[12] Mark 16:15,16.

[13] 1 Peter 1:7.

[14] 1 Peter 4:12.

[15] Acts 2:4.

[16] Ephesians 5:19.

[17] Revelation 1:13.

[18] John 12:32.

[19] 19th Century hymn; words and music by Margaret J. Harris.

[20] Judson W. Van de Venter, 1855-1939. The song was composed as a testimony to the author's five-year struggle preceding his decision to surrender a promising career as an artist and art teacher in order to spend his life in full-time Christian ministry.

[21] Psalm 139:23.

[22] Isaiah 1:18.

[23] Psalm 103:10-12.

[24] 1 John 1:9.

[25] 1 John 1:7.

[26] 1 Corinthians 11:25.

[27] Matthew 26:27.

[28] Words by Isaac Watts, written in 1707 for use in a Communion service he conducted; melody from a Gregorian Chant, arranged by Lowell Mason.

[29] Words and music by Andrae Crouch.

[30] Words and music by Thoro Harris, 1874-1955.

# 12

# You Are Invited *

The presbyters are distributing among you little memorial folders, prepared to remind us this morning that we are gathered here in memory of our Lord and Savior, Jesus Christ, to remind ourselves of the price He paid for our redemption and the promise of His return. May I suggest that you put this folder in your Bible after we finish with it here this morning, so that as you see it from time to time you will be reminded of the price . . . and the promise.[1]

"*When the hour came, Jesus and his apostles reclined at the table. And he said to them, 'I have eagerly desired to eat this Passover with you before I suffer. For I tell you, I will not eat it again until it finds fulfillment in the kingdom of God.'*

"*After taking the cup, he gave thanks and said, 'Take this and divide it among you. For I tell you I will not drink again of the fruit of the vine until the kingdom of God comes.'*

"*And he took bread, gave thanks and broke it, and gave it to them, saying, 'This is my body given for you; do this in remembrance of me.'*

"*In the same way, after the supper he took the cup, saying, 'This cup is the new covenant in my blood, which is poured out for you. But the hand of him who is going to betray me is with mine on the table. The Son of man will go as it has been decreed, but woe to that man who betrays him.' They began*

---

* Sermon for the Communion Service of the 1996 Ohio District Council of the Assemblies of God, Tri County Assembly of God, Fairfield, Ohio.

*to question among themselves which of them it might be who would do this.*

*"Also a dispute arose among them as to which of them was considered to be the greatest. Jesus said to them, 'The kings of the Gentiles lord it over them; and those who exercise authority over them call themselves Benefactors. But you are not to be like that. Instead, the greatest among you should be like the youngest, and the one who rules like the one who serves.*

*"'For who is greater, the one who is at the table or the one who serves? Is it not the one who is at the table? But I am among you as one who serves. You are those who have stood by me in my trials. And I confer on you a kingdom, just as my Father conferred one on me, so that you may eat and drink at my table in my kingdom and sit on thrones, judging the twelve tribes of Israel.*

*"'Simon, Simon, Satan has asked to sift you as wheat. But I have prayed for you, Simon, that your faith may not fail. And when you have turned back, strengthen your brothers.'*

*"But he replied, 'Lord, I am ready to go with you to prison and to death.'*

*"Jesus answered, 'I tell you, Peter, before the rooster crows today, you will deny three times that you know me.'"*[2]

### The price . . . and the promise

Jesus was about to pay a terrible, awesome *price* for our salvation. We need to be mindful of that. But we also need to remember the *promise* He made. He was not going away from them forever. The separation would be temporary, because He would bring them to be with Him and they would share the Passover observance together when it found fulfillment in the kingdom of God. He offered them the bread and the cup and promised that He would partake of the bread which represented His body and *"drink again of the fruit of the vine [when] the kingdom of God comes."* He promised to *"confer on you a kingdom, just as my Father conferred one on me, so that you may eat and drink at my table in my kingdom and sit on thrones."* But first, He would endure pain, betrayal, humiliation, and suffering such as no one had ever endured.

Now let's look at some of what Jesus soon revealed about the *promise* to the apostle John, who was in exile on the Island of Patmos (Greece):

> *"Then I heard what sounded like a great multitude, like the roar of rushing waters and like loud peals of thunder, shouting: 'Hallelujah! For our Lord God Almighty reigns. Let us rejoice and be glad and give him glory! For the wedding of the Lamb has come, and his bride has made herself ready. Fine linen, bright and clean, was given her to wear.' (Fine linen stands for the righteous acts of the saints.)*
>
> *"Then the angel said to me, 'Write: "Blessed are those who are invited to the wedding supper of the Lamb!"' And he added, 'These are the true words of God.'*
>
> *"At this I fell at his feet to worship him. But he said to me, 'Do not do it! I am a fellow servant with you and with your brothers who hold to the testimony of Jesus. Worship God! For the testimony of Jesus is the spirit of prophecy.'*
>
> *"I saw heaven standing open and there before me was a white horse, whose rider is called Faithful and True. With justice he judges and makes war. His eyes are like blazing fire, and on his head are many crowns. He has a name written on him that no one knows but he himself. He is dressed in a robe dipped in blood, and his name is the Word of God. The armies of heaven were following him, riding on white horses and dressed in fine linen, white and clean.*
>
> *"Out of his mouth comes a sharp sword with which to strike down the nations. 'He will rule them with an iron scepter.' He treads the winepress of the fury of the wrath of God Almighty. On his robe and on his thigh he has this name written, KING OF KINGS AND LORD OF LORDS.*[3]

Let's bow our hearts in prayer.

*Father, this is a special time in which we come to You as part of Your family. We reflect upon 50 years of the faithful servanthood of those whose lives have been sown in Your kingdom across this state, this nation, and around the world, as our Ohio District approaches its 50th anniversary. We thank you for those who have stood before us and shouldered the burden of leadership as our District Superintendents: Brother Clem Van Meter, Brother Bond, Brother James Van Meter, Brother Hahn, Brother Parsons, and now our Brother Crabtree. We thank You for their faithful leadership.*

*And we pray, as we pause on our journey today, that You will help us to properly reflect so that the moments we spend around Your Table might be special moments. May they make an impact and a difference in our lives, our marriages, and our families. For these really are our ministries; it matters little what those outside the family think of us if our lives do not bear witness to our family that Christ lives within us.*

*Help us this morning to judge ourselves and our need for cleansing, so that Communion may be a source of life; of health and healing; of strength and power to us. Help us to approach this time together so that it might intensify the bond between our heart and Yours, Lord, and among our hearts as brothers and sisters in Christ. These things we pray in Jesus' Name. Amen.*

All four gospels record our Lord's celebration of the last Passover feast with His disciples. These accounts are found in Matthew 26, Mark 14, Luke 22 (our text today), and John 13. Although Jesus had celebrated previous Passovers with His disciples, there was something very special about this one. This was to be His last on earth, and He made special arrangements for this Passover. He extended a special invitation for His disciples to join Him, which Luke's account we read earlier clearly records: *"I have eagerly desired to eat this Passover with you before I suffer. For I tell you, I will not eat it again until it finds fulfillment in the kingdom of God."*

At the end of this very special Passover meal, Jesus presented the symbols He had chosen to remind His followers of His sacrificial death: the bread and the cup. One at a time, He took these emblems in His hands as He led the disciples in the very first celebration of Christian Communion. In 1 Corinthians 11:23-26, Paul reminds us that every time we come to the Lord's Table, we are here because He has invited us here. Paul reminds us that this should be a very special time for us, just as it was for that early group of believers. As the disciples celebrated their first Christian Communion, their attention was focused in three directions. They looked back, they looked around and inside themselves at that moment, and they looked ahead.

## Look back at your heritage of faith

At Passover, the Jewish disciples looked back to that night in their history when Moses led their forefathers in slaying a spotless, unblemished lamb and sprinkling its blood on the door posts of every home in Goshen, to protect Israel's firstborn children from the death angel. That was the night the death angel broke the will of a stubborn Pharaoh by killing the firstborn of every Egyptian family. It was the night in history when the children of Israel were finally set free from the bondage of Egyptian slavery and began their exodus from Egypt toward the Promised Land, led by a cloud of smoke in the daytime and a pillar of fire by night.

Jesus helped the disciples at that first Communion observance to look back even further, to that moment in eternity past when He chose to answer the Father's call on His life. He reminded them that He chose to put down the rebellion of Lucifer.

He chose to take upon himself the form of a servant. He chose to become obedient to the Father, even though it would mean His death on the cross. He chose to become the Lamb of God, " . . . *slain from the foundation of the world.* "[4] The disciples looked back. Jesus looked back. And I would suggest this morning that, as we approach this special moment with our Lord, you and I need to look back to that time in our lives when we were still servants of sin.

There has not always been a title in front of our names that identifies us as full-time ministers of the gospel of Jesus Christ. We have not always been esteemed highly enough among the Body of Christ to be delegated to a convention such as this. Many of us fail to acknowledge frequently—or ever— what we were before Jesus found us. Although I was saved and filled with the Holy Spirit in one glorious experience when I was not quite sixteen years old, I knew I was a sinner. I knew I had taken the Lord's name in vain. I knew I had been dishonest. I knew I had lasciviousness in my heart and licentiousness in my spirit before He cleaned up my heart and my life.

We need to look back this morning, to remind ourselves of who we were before we came to that first spiritual communion with Christ, before we were changed by the regenerating power of the Holy Spirit. Our children and grandchildren, second- and third-generation heirs of a Christian heritage, need to hear us say publicly who we were before Jesus came into our lives. They need to hear about the difference Jesus Christ made in the way we lived, the way we related to our husband or wife in marriage, and the difference in the way we went about raising our families from the way some of us were raised.

The Israelites' descendants still celebrate Passover because they don't want to forget who they were and where they were before God so miraculously delivered them from slavery in Egypt. And as we come to the Table of the Lord this morning, we need to take a look back, just as the disciples with Jesus that evening looked back at where they had been. We need to look back to the time when Jesus baptized us with the Holy Spirit, when our pride was thoroughly trampled in sweat and tears. I remember the times when I went home from church on Sunday night with the sleeves of my white shirt gray from carpet dust, where I'd flailed my arms in spiritual hunger and desperation as God worked out His sanctifying presence in my life. We need to remember those times.

### Look back at your spiritual experience

We need to remember how simple it was when we finally allowed our spirit to bypass our intelligence and pray with the Spirit of God in a language that God gave us, a language that could not be taught or shaken into us by some over-zealous saint. We need to remember those times when we were admonished to *hang on and let go*; times when, finally, we learned that the Holy Spirit is Jesus' gift to the Church and He baptized us with the Holy Spirit.

I do *not* want to be numbered among those who will deny that the initial physical evidence of the Baptism of the Holy Spirit is speaking in other tongues. My heart is grieved to think that 50 percent of the members of Assemblies of God churches live without the daily edification of speaking in a language that only the Spirit can enable them to express. We need to look back.

We need to look back to the times when Jesus healed us and extended our lives for His glory. We need to remember the times that He broke through in impossible moments in our personal lives, our families, and our congregational experiences.

## Look back at your calling

Each of us in the ministry needs to remember the time when Christ called us to this task. Fifty years ago this month, in 1946, the Illinois District Council of the Assemblies of God licensed me to preach the gospel. That was in confirmation of the call God had put on my life two years earlier. Three years later, in 1949, that same District Council would ordain me to the ministry as the hands of W. I. Evans were placed on my head.

Let me say to our ordination candidates that the presbyter who lays hands on you tonight will have laid hands on many other young men and young women to ordain them to ministry. It's highly unlikely that W. I. Evans remembers laying hands on me. *But I vividly remember that experience* just as I remember the time when God made it clear to me that He was calling me into the ministry. Likewise, you will remember for the rest of your life the man who lays hands on you tonight and symbolically—as our Lord would do if He were physically here—seals the lifetime covenant you are making with your heavenly Father. *The disciples took a look back.*

## Look around and within yourself

The disciples also took a look around. Seated among the twelve at the Table of the Lord were one who would betray Him and one who would deny even knowing Him.

When Jesus said that one of them would betray Him, the disciples began to inquire among themselves as to who this might possibly be. Both Jesus and Judas knew the identity of the betrayer; the others wondered aloud. One of them was in total disbelief that *anyone* could do such a thing. Another, who was perhaps more honest than most, said, *Am I the one?* This moment of agonizing inquiry is what Leonardo da Vinci chose to capture in his world-famous painting of The Last Supper. He painted it on the wall of a monastery dining hall near Milan, Italy, where men who had made a lifetime commitment to Christian service would see it every day. They, too, would have the opportunity to examine themselves by looking inside their own lives and asking themselves, every time they saw that masterful painting, *Have I betrayed You today, Lord? Have I denied You today?*

Judas is seated on Christ's right side in da Vinci's painting, with only the apostle John sitting between himself and Jesus. His face is in the shadows—he doesn't have to ask anybody anything. The pouch of money is tightly clasped in his hand. We of the Arminian branch of Protestant Christendom believe that, even at the time of the Last Supper, Judas still had the opportunity to repent. He still could have refused to go through with his betrayal of the Lord. That very first Communion observance provided all the opportunity he needed. However, Judas spurned the grace that could have been his at that moment. He turned his back on the Lord and went about his bloody business.

John makes an interesting observation about this in the 13th chapter of his Gospel, stating that, *"... it was night"* after Judas accepted the sop from Jesus ("sop" was a piece of food that had been dipped in liquid). John's words here are of far more importance than just noting the time of day when this event happened. He is commenting on the spiritual condition of the man who would betray their Lord for money.

As Jesus continued His examination of the disciples' spiritual condition, he predicted that Peter would deny Him. Peter is portrayed by da Vinci as leaning around behind Judas and talking to John, perhaps asking *him* to reaffirm to Jesus that Peter wouldn't ever deny Him. Peter insisted that he was ready to go to prison and even to death for his Lord. But Jesus knew Peter's heart better than Peter did. He knew it so well that He could predict the very hour when Peter would deny Him.

**Judas wouldn't be honest . . . Peter couldn't be honest**

Neither Judas nor Peter was able to be honest about the condition of his own heart at this first Communion. Judas *wouldn't* be honest. He'd already struck his ruthless bargain. And Peter *couldn't* be honest because he was still so spiritually blind that he couldn't see what the Lord knew to be true about him.

Everyone who has ever known and then betrayed the Lord; everyone who has ever known and then denied the Lord; has had the opportunity to take part in a Communion observance such as we come to this morning, invited there by the Lord. These men and women have simply sat there and neglected the opportunity for self-examination that could have spared them such a tragedy. Self-examination is one of the main purposes of Communion.

## Look to the future

It's highly probable that some among us this morning will deny the Lord. That's an ominous and solemn thought, but if you understand much about the human heart's true nature, then you know I'm telling you the truth. And it's quite probable, in a group of ministers and lay leaders of this number, that some here are too prideful to confess and forsake the secret thoughts and behaviors that are dragging them down and will eventually destroy their Christian witness.

We all know what it is to hear the sad news that a fellow laborer has experienced moral failure. We can't help but wonder what could have been going through his or her mind at those moments when they approached the Table of the Lord—the place where they could have confessed their shortcomings *before the crowing of the rooster.* Before they were publicly humiliated and lost the privilege of ministering to the Body of Christ. What was so important to them that the invitation of our Lord to examine themselves was set aside for some other agenda?

## Beware of unhealthy ambition

There was also controversy among the disciples about who among them should be considered most important. We're a strange crowd, we Pentecostals. The Scriptures do say, *"If a man desire the office of a bishop, he desireth a good thing."*[5] However, if unhealthy ambition for personal gain is evident, it will seldom, if ever, be fulfilled among us. God knows our ambitions. He knows the motives of our heart. He knows the many times we look at leadership and say, "I could do it better than that." He knows when our prayer requests are really disguised criticism or an opportunity to gossip.

He will show us all of this and more about ourselves if we will accept His invitation this morning. That's why He has invited us here: to show us our hearts and to cleanse and purify them; to spare us moments of denial, embarrassment, and shame. And the wise among us will examine ourselves today. We will not forsake the truth of His Word to subscribe to the myth that Christians do not sin. We will know that if we say we have not sinned, we are only deceiving ourselves.

Please don't ask me to believe that no one among us today has some private, personal ambition. Do you remember the old talent contests and the vocabulary that was necessary to win? I remember it well: "We don't have any talent at all. It's all Jesus; pray that He will just keep us hidden behind the cross so that only He will shine through. We don't take any of the credit for what He does through us." No matter what the category or the presentation, the contestants willing to use that kind of vocabulary always took the trophy. *(All you would have had to do to test their sincerity would be to agree with them. Of course, they would be really rankled by your agreement, but what could they say? They'd already claimed they had no talent!)*

At times we all adopt a vocabulary that veils our ambitions. But God sees the unveiled heart. He knows far more about us than we are able to receive. And if we will submit ourselves to Him this morning, He'll cleanse our sins and sanctify our ambitions.

#### Ambition in and of itself is neutral . . .

Ambition is not necessarily a bad thing; it has the potential for good or evil, depending on how it's directed. But it needs to be submitted to the Lordship of Jesus: *"But he that is greatest among you shall be your servant."*[6] John records the very graphic lesson on servant leadership that Jesus taught when He wrapped himself with a towel and washed His disciples' feet, urging them likewise to wash one another's feet. May God make us encouragers of one another. May He build a brotherhood among us that helps us to strengthen one another, to lift and encourage one another, to affirm one another.

At the first Communion service, the disciples took a look *back*. They also took a look *around*, and a look *ahead*. Although this may have been the *first time* Jesus shared the bread and the cup with His disciples at a Passover celebration, it would not be the *last*. Luke 22:16 (NIV) shares His words with us: *"For I tell you, I will not eat it again until it finds fulfillment in the kingdom of God."* Jesus promised His followers, because they were faithful to stand by Him in His hour of trial, that when He inherited the kingdom His Father had prepared for Him He would likewise assign part of that kingdom to them. They would eat and drink at His table in His kingdom. They would be seated on thrones, judging the twelve tribes of Israel.

Every celebration of Communion should anticipate that moment when we will finally hear, " . . . *A voice from heaven, as the voice of many waters, and as the voice of a great thunder . . . the voice of harpers harping with their harps . . ..*"[7] We will hear the voices singing, *"Hallelujah! For our Lord God Almighty reigns. Let us rejoice and be glad and give him glory! For the wedding of the Lamb has come, and his bride has made herself ready."*[8]

### Preparing for the Marriage Supper of the lamb

Each of us needs to do whatever is necessary to get ready for that wedding banquet. By the time we are seated at that glorious Marriage Supper of the Lamb, we will already have been to the Judgment Seat of Christ. We will have seen how wrong we were to think He never noticed what we did in His Name. We will discover that *every cup of cold water* we have given to someone with the right motive will be counted to our credit. Those times when we felt little or no affirmation from fellow believers or ministry friends, very little recognition from our fellowship, will prove to be times when Christ was there. We will realize that He saw what we did for Him.

If we have sown bountifully, we will reap bountifully. Some will walk away from the Judgment Seat of Christ, having had their works tried by fire, with only their eternal souls and nothing else to lay at His feet. They will discover that their life on earth was merely a heap of ashes. Others will find that their works truly built something of Kingdom value; that they were of gold and silver and precious stones. For these believers, all of the trials and tribulations during their earthly years will be worth whatever they had to endure once they see Jesus and hear His voice say to them, *Well done, my good and faithful servant.*

In the words of the hymn writer . . .

". . . Life's trials will seem so small when we see Christ.
One glimpse of His dear face all sorrows will erase.
So gladly run the race, 'til we see Christ."[9]

That great Marriage Supper of the Lamb to which we have been invited is such a great event that the angel instructed John to write,

*"Blessed are they which are called unto the marriage supper of the Lamb
. . . these are the true sayings of God."*[10]

As we approach the Table of the Lord this morning, let's remind
ourselves of where we were and who we were before Christ came into
our life as Savior and Lord. Let's us remind ourselves how hard it was
for our stammering lips to break through to a prayer language so we
could express ourselves "spirit to spirit" with God. Let's celebrate that
liberty this morning as we approach the Table of the Lord.

As we look around at our number, we need to realize that some
of us here today will undoubtedly fail the Lord and deny Him unless
each of us accepts His solemn invitation to examine ourselves privately
in His presence. However, none who are here at His Table need to leave
afraid of failure if our hearts are open to Him, cleansed with His blood,
and strengthened by His Spirit. May each of us determine that we are
not going to be that one who will betray or deny the Lord. May we
purposefully and regularly examine ourselves in His presence.

### Empowerment at the Table of the Lord

The disciples left that first Communion service to become
witnesses of our Lord's crucifixion and resurrection. Fifty days after the
resurrection, they launched the building of His Church on the Day of
Pentecost. When the work of the Church on earth is finished and we
leave the Marriage Supper of the Lamb, we will return with Jesus to set
up His millennial kingdom on this earth. John describes it this way:

*"And I saw heaven opened, and behold a white horse; and he
that sat upon him was called Faithful and True, and in righteousness he
doth judge and make war. His eyes were as a flame of fire, and on his
head were many crowns; and he had a name written, that no man knew,
but he himself. And he was clothed with a vesture dipped in blood: and
his name is called The Word of God.*

*"And the armies which were in heaven followed him upon white
horses, clothed in fine linen, white and clean. And out of his mouth goeth
a sharp sword, that with it he should smite the nations: and he shall rule
them with a rod of iron: and he treadeth the winepress of the fierceness
and wrath of Almighty God. And he hath on his vesture and on his thigh
a name written, KING OF KINGS, AND LORD OF LORDS."*[11]

The One Who invites us to His Table this morning to examine ourselves also invites us to the Marriage Supper of the Lamb. Following that banquet, He invites us to return from that glorious moment of victory to rule and reign with Him for a thousand years. You are invited.

Shall we bow our hearts in prayer.

*Father, this morning as we come to You, help us to use the next few moments of this service meaningfully. You know the agenda the Holy Spirit would have each one of us personally address. May we spend more time looking inward this morning than looking around . . . show each of us what we need to examine in our own lives. As the disciples who sat with You, Lord Jesus, in that first Communion service, asked of themselves and each other, help each of us to identify those things in our lives that would deny or betray You. We need to feel something of the same emotion they felt when they were stunned by Your words that one of them would deny and one would betray You. May each of us ask ourselves privately, this morning, Lord, is it me? Am I the one?* "Search me, O God, and know my heart: try me, and know my thoughts: And see if there be any wicked way in me, and lead me in the way everlasting."[12] *In Jesus' Name we pray, Amen.*

(Congregational singing: "Glory to the Lamb.")

As we are being served, let's anticipate the breaking of the bread. If you are here in good health, reflect on the goodness of God. And then reflect upon those in your family and among your local congregation who are going through severe tests in their physical body. If you are here in need of healing, think about how His body was broken so that ours might be made whole. In that moment when we take the bread, we will celebrate health and claim the Holy Spirit's gifts of healing among our number this morning. Hallelujah! We praise you, Lord. And let's bow our hearts in prayer once again.

*Our bodies are so frail, Lord. Sometimes, in the arrogance of our fallen nature, we claim life we do not have. Humble us this morning. Teach us the wisdom of planning our tomorrows in accordance with the way you taught us to think and pray:* " . . . Thy will be done,"[13] *for we don't know what tomorrow will bring. O God, let the young and the healthy be even more strengthened in the eating of the bread, that Your*

*Son, Jesus Christ, might have vigorous expression in their bodies among those with whom they live and serve.*

*Others of us today are struggling with bodies that are showing the results of time; bodies that are feeling the weakness of disease. Help us remember Your promise that, "* . . . These signs shall follow them that believe; In my name shall they cast out devils; they shall speak with new tongues . . . they shall lay hands on the sick, and they shall recover."[14] *We know that one of the gifts the Spirit distributes "severally as He will"[15] is described as* "gifts of healing." *Let healing waters flow among us.*

*Jesus was "* . . . wounded for our transgressions; he was bruised for our iniquities: the chastisement of our peace was upon him; and with his stripes we are healed."[16] *May those gifts of healing be distributed this morning, Lord. Wherever Your Name can be glorified, let it be glorified in our bodies, whether by life or by death:* "For to me to live is Christ, and to die is gain."[17] *These things we pray in Jesus' Name. Amen.*

*" . . . The Lord Jesus, the same night in which he was betrayed took bread: And when he had given thanks, he brake it, and said, Take, eat: this is my body, which is broken for you: this do in remembrance of me."[18]*

Shall we eat together. And let's praise Him for health and life and healing.

*Father, You said that as we approach the Table of the Lord, we should examine ourselves. It's so difficult to keep our mind on the moment at hand so that we might indeed examine ourselves. The anxieties of life . . . our responsibilities . . . our dreams . . . our visions . . . these things so quickly and easily distract us, taking our minds away from examining our hearts and into other concerns. Help us to focus on the Lamb this morning. Help us to focus on His eyes—which are like flames of fire—as He sees into us more deeply than we can ever see into ourselves.*

*And help us to pray as David prayed,* "Search me, O God, and know my heart: try me, and know my thoughts.[19] *I confess my sins to You this morning, Lord Jesus. As I stand here among my brothers and sisters, I ask You to forgive me for pride and ambition that are not becoming to You. Forgive me, Lord, for letting my priorities stray from the focus of Your Word. Oh, God, help me not be deceived into believing*

*that I have no sin. But assure me of Your forgiveness and cleansing, just
as You help me to be honest enough to confess my sin. In Jesus' Name,
Amen.*

Shall we drink the cup together.

[1] 1 Corinthians 6:20; John 3:16,17.
[2] Luke 22:14-34, NIV.
[3] Revelation 19:6-16, NIV.
[4] Revelation 13:8.
[5] 1 Timothy 3:1.
[6] Matthew 23:11.
[7] Revelation 14:2.
[8] Revelation 19:6,7.
[9] Esther Rusthoi, 1909-1962, ©1941 by Singspiration, Inc.
[10] Revelation 19:9.
[11] Revelation 19:11-16.
[12] Psalm 139:23,24.
[13] Matthew 6:10.
[14] Mark 16:17,18.
[15] 1 Corinthians 12:7-11.
[16] Isaiah 53:5.
[17] Philippians 1:21.
[18] 1 Corinthians 11:23,24.
[19] Psalm 139:23.

# 13

# Personal Examination in Preparing for Communion *

I was determined that this year I would sit where I could see the pictures of our fellow ministers who have gone to be with the Lord since our last District Council. We never know when our picture is going to be included in this memorial service. I think one of the things that make us such poor stewards of life is our insistence on denying our death. For, life comes to us in limited length. We begin to die the day we are born. Discovering the value of each day and celebrating it as unto the Lord is a secret that comes to many of us far later in life than it ought.

Incidentally, our friends whose pictures we have seen here are not dead. They are very much alive and in the presence of the Lord.[1] Sin and death have no more dominion over them . . . nor will we be within the reach of sin and death when we are in His presence!

As I stood recently in a mausoleum where one of the Lord's choicest servants was about to be laid to rest, I thought about the creative genius of moviemakers like Steven Spielberg who can give us a story about recombinant DNA resurrecting a forest of frightening dinosaurs. If that were true, perhaps God would need a DNA sample from the dust of our earthly bodies order to make those bodies spring to life when the trumpet sounds. However, Paul said it . . . and I believe it . . . *"Why should any of you consider it incredible that God raises the dead?"*[2] All God has to do is speak the word . . . no DNA needed! Hallelujah!

---

* Sermon for the Communion Service of the 1997 Ohio District Council of the Assemblies of God, Faith Memorial Assembly of God, Sandusky, Ohio.

Now let's turn our thoughts toward Communion. I'm asking you to indulge me this morning. On this occasion when we probably should be reading the most formal of Bible translations, we're going to read from The Living Bible. But I think during the course of our reading you will understand why I wanted to use this translation. Let's read 1 Corinthians 11:17-33 (TLB):

*"Next on my list of items to write you about is something else I cannot agree with. For it sounds as if more harm than good is done when you meet together for your communion services. Everyone keeps telling me about the arguing that goes on in these meetings and the divisions developing among you, and I can just about believe it. But I suppose you feel this is necessary so that you who are always right will become known and recognized.*

*"When you come together to eat, it isn't the Lord's Supper you are eating, but your own. For I am told that everyone hastily gobbles all the food he can without waiting to share with the others, so that one doesn't get enough and goes hungry while another has too much to drink and gets drunk. What! Is this really true? Can't you do your eating and drinking at home, to avoid disgracing the church and shaming those who are poor and can bring no food? What am I supposed to say about these things? Do you want me to praise you? Well, I certainly do not!*

*"For this is what the Lord himself has said about his Table, and I have passed it on to you before: That on the night when Judas betrayed him, the Lord Jesus took bread, and when he had given thanks to God for it, he broke it and gave it to his disciples and said, 'Take this and eat it. This is my body which is given for you. Do this to remember me.'*

*"In the same way, he took the cup of wine after supper, saying, 'This cup is the new agreement between God and you that has been established and set in motion by my blood. Do this in remembrance of me whenever you drink it.' For every time you eat this bread and drink this cup, you are re-telling the message of the Lord's death, that he has died for you. Do this until he comes again.*

*"So if anyone eats this bread and drinks from this cup of the Lord in an unworthy manner, he is guilty of sin against the body and blood of the Lord. That is why a man should examine himself carefully before eating the bread and drinking from the cup. For if he eats the*

*bread and drinks from the cup unworthily, not thinking about the body of Christ and what it means, he is eating and drinking God's judgment upon himself; for he is trifling with the death of Christ. That is why many of you are weak and sick and some have even died.*

*"But if you carefully examine yourselves before eating you will not need to be judged and punished. Yet, when we are judged and punished by the Lord, it is so that we will not be condemned with the rest of the world. So, dear brothers, when you gather for the Lord's Supper—the Communion Service—wait for each other."*

Let's conclude our Scripture reading with 1 Corinthians 12:27 (TLB): *"Now here is what I am trying to say: All of you together are the one body of Christ and each one of you is a separate and necessary part of it."*

Shall we pray.

*Father, we thank You for Jesus Christ, for He is the head of all things. He is the Head of the Church. I thank You for my brothers and sisters here today, for those You have placed in leadership over us, and for those who serve with us. Help us to understand that not one of us is more important or less important than any other. For we are all members of the Body of Christ. When one of us is unhealthy, it affects the function of the whole Body. And when each of us is healthy, it presents a vigorous Body through which You can express Your life on earth.*

*Anoint us this morning, for we are so dependent on the anointing of the Holy Spirit. Help me to say what You want me to say, and help us to hear what You want us to hear, as we prepare our hearts to receive Communion. In Jesus' Name, Amen.*

### Communion is a celebration of deliverance

The Christian ordinance of Communion is rooted in the Jewish celebration of Passover, a feast which commemorates their deliverance from the bondage of Egyptian slavery. When the midnight flight of the death angel broke Pharaoh's stubborn resistance and freed the Hebrew slaves, it was the blood of the perfect lamb sprinkled above the Hebrews' doorposts that spared the firstborn of Israel. All of the firstborn of Egypt, human and animal alike, were killed, but the death angel "passed over" the Hebrews' homes. Every year since then, in commemoration of that terrifying and awesome night, Jews all over the world have celebrated the Feast of Passover.

Before our Lord Jesus was crucified, He sent His disciples to prepare for this feast so He could celebrate it with them. Matthew 26:19 (TLB) says, *"So the disciples did as He told them, and prepared the supper there."*

### Preparing for the Passover

On Thursday morning, they would have prepared unleavened (flat) bread and taken care to see that every trace of leaven was removed from the house. Why would they have made unleavened bread for the Passover feast? First, it was to remind them of the speed with which God brought deliverance to them. When the time came to leave Egypt, it came in a hurry. After much stalling and going back on his promises, Pharaoh, on the dreadful night of the death angel's visit, finally said "Go." The Israelites left Egypt in such a hurry there was no time to make regular bread dough with yeast and let it properly rise. The unleavened bread was to remind them of the speed with which God delivered them.

Second, leaven also had come to represent what was sinful and corrupt to those of the Jewish faith. For this reason, the house was to be totally rid of leaven and they were to eat unleavened bread with the Passover.

On Thursday afternoon, the disciples—all of whom were Jews— would have taken a lamb to the temple, had it slain, and offered its blood to God as a sacrifice for their sins. Then they would have prepared its meat for the Passover feast.

They would also have prepared four special things for the Passover table as other reminders of their forefathers' experience. First, they would have made a bowl of salt water to remind them of the tears the Hebrews had shed as slaves in Egypt and the waters of the Red Sea through which God's hand had miraculously delivered them. Second, they would have prepared a collection of bitter herbs to remind them of their slavery and of the branch of hyssop with which the blood of the lamb had been smeared on the lentil and door posts the night of their deliverance. (Hyssop branches were commonly used to sprinkle water in Jewish purification rites.) Third, they would have made the charoset, a paste consisting of apples, dates, pomegranates, nuts, and sticks of cinnamon. Charoset symbolized the clay and straw from which the Hebrews were forced to make bricks in Egypt. Finally, they would place four cups of wine on the table to remind them of the four promises God made to Israel in Exodus 6:6,7: *"[1] I will bring you out from under the burdens of the Egyptians, and [2] I will rid you out of their bondage, and [3] I will redeem you with a stretched out arm, and with great judgments; [4] And I will take you to me for a people, and I will be to you a God."*

This was the task Jesus commanded His disciples to carry out. And once these things were in place, He and His disciples gathered on the 15th day of the Jewish month of Nisan to celebrate the Passover. After celebrating this *memorial feast of the Old Covenant* with His disciples, Jesus initiated the Lord's Supper—the *memorial feast of God's New Covenant.*

**God made the old covenant with sinners . . .**
**Jesus made the new covenant with sinners.**

In the Old Covenant, the blood of a lamb was spilled. In the New Covenant, the blood of God's only begotten Son, *the Lamb of God,* Who was *"slain from [before] the foundation of the world,*[3] was spilled. It was at the end of the Passover meal that Jesus took bread and wine and instituted the memorial feast of God's New Covenant with sinners, sealed by our Lord's broken body and shed blood. This is what we have come to call the Lord's Supper or Communion.

At this first Lord's Supper, Jesus announced His betrayal and His death to the disciples. These were shocking words for them to hear. With one exception, they were stunned to think that He would die. They were even more incredulous that one of *them* would betray Him. Immediately, from all around the table, they began to ask, "Lord, is it I? Who would do such a thing? Is it I? Is it I?" They were making themselves accountable to Him; asking Him to look farther inside them than they could see for themselves, to determine whether they had betrayed or denied Him.

Among the great theological truths symbolized by Communion, none looms larger than the need to hold oneself accountable to God. As we personally prepare ourselves for Communion today by examining our hearts, let us remind ourselves of all the ways we are accountable. We are accountable to God, to our local church body, and the Body of Christ in heaven as well as on earth.

### Examining who we were

In 1 Corinthians 11:28,31, Paul says we should examine ourselves very carefully before eating the Bread and drinking the Cup. I would like to suggest three ways in which we should examine ourselves this morning. First of all, each of us needs to examine his or her relationship with God. I cannot do that for you. You cannot do that for me. Paul emphasizes this when he calls the Corinthians to self-examination by also making it clear that it is necessary for him to consider his own sins.

This morning and every time we examine ourselves in preparation for Communion, we need to remember our own pre-conversion sins. This is something we need to do frequently during times of self-examination, to keep us grateful to God for the difference Jesus has made in our lives.

*Paul never forgot his pre-conversion sins.* We know he forgot the condemnation they brought to him, because he tells us that in Philippians 3:13: *" . . . But this one thing I do, forgetting those things which are behind . . .."* However, it's clear that he remembers what he did before he met the Master. In 1 Timothy 1:15, he says, *" . . . Christ Jesus came into the world to save sinners; of whom I am chief."*

Paul never allowed himself to forget where he came from or how fiercely he persecuted the early Christians by consigning them to prison and killing them. He had made widows of *many* Christian men's wives and orphans of their children.[4] Although we don't often sing it any more, I still like the refrain, "What a wonderful change in my life has been wrought, Since Jesus came into my heart!"[5]

Reminding ourselves of our pre-conversion sins keeps us humble and honest about our present sins, just as it did Paul. Remembering where we've come from helps us be truly thankful for the wonderful change Jesus has brought about in us.

### Examining who we are

Paul shares his own current struggle with sin in Romans chapters 6 and 7, before he leads us into that glorious, triumphant 8th chapter of Romans, which starts out with this jubilant reminder:

*"There is therefore now no condemnation to them which are in Christ Jesus, who walk not after the flesh, but after the Spirit. For the law of the Spirit of life in Christ Jesus hath made me free from the law of sin and death. For what the law could not do, in that it was weak through the flesh, God sending his own Son in the likeness of sinful flesh, and for sin, condemned sin in the flesh: That the righteousness of the law might be fulfilled in us, who walk not after the flesh, but after the Spirit."*[6]

And in 1 Corinthians 9:27, he says that he is determined to keep his body under subjection to the Lordship of Christ in order to avoid those sins that will result in him becoming a castaway. And the symbolism there is not that of a lost person, but of a pen that has become so blunted the author can no longer use it for writing.

At EMERGE we see many servants of God who have been gifted with tremendous ministries . . . but who no longer remember their pre-conversion sins. They compound this carelessness by deceiving themselves about their present sins to the point that they sin away their usefulness to the Body of Christ. They can still be saved. They can still have a ministry to the Body of Christ. But they lose the ministry to which God has called them and to which they once dedicated their lives. And the loss of that ministry begins the first time they take Communion without first asking God for forgiveness for sins they know they've committed. When we take Communion under those circumstances, we begin the process of hardening our hearts. God alone knows how many ministers officiate at Communion services, baptize believers, preach sermons, and pray for the sick *when their own private lives harbor unconfessed personal sins.* We should examine ourselves, first of all in our relationship with God.

The Greek word for *examine* in 1 Corinthians 11:28 implies *having been tested and found true.* Paul is saying that before we take Communion, we should examine ourselves in order to take care of any necessary confession or repentance so that we may take Communion as *one having been tested and found true.* If careful examination reveals we have not been true, then the Table of the Lord is an opportunity for confession and cleansing. However, when we fail to examine ourselves carefully before we take Communion, we initiate a hardening of our conscience that inevitably precedes shipwreck of the soul. Let us not approach the Lord's Table thoughtlessly.

### ➔ Our focus should be on ourselves, not others

And, let us not approach His Table with an eye on what others have been doing . . . what we think they should be doing here today because of what we believe they have been doing lately. . . what's going on in their heart . . . none of this is any of our business. *Our business is what's going on between us and God personally.* Let's take a lesson from the disciples: Is it I? Let's examine ourselves in our relationship with God as we prepare to take Communion.

Second, let's examine our own self in our relationship with others in our church. Notice 1 Corinthians 11:27 (TLB), *"So if anyone eats this bread and drinks from this cup of the Lord in an unworthy manner, he is guilty of sin against the body and the blood of the Lord."* Christ and the church form one Body. And until we are in a right relationship with other members of the Body, there is an ailment in that Body that cripples the Lord's ability to use the Body for His kingdom.

The devil does not care how big your church gets, as long as he can keep it divided. Unity is what makes him tremble. Not size. And let me say to those pastors and board members here today*, you have no higher responsibility than keeping your local church body united.* Endeavoring to keep the unity of the Spirit in the bonds of peace is the highest responsibility of a pastor and a board. And when your church divides, both the pastor and the board have failed in this area and you need to share responsibility for it. For when one member of the Body of Christ has been separated from another member or members, there is no vital flow to join them in a common effort to express Christ to the community.

Christ and the church form one Body. He is the Head; we are the members. Christ and the Church are to exist in organic unity. We are members of His Body; His blood gives us life. The only life we have as a Church is the life His blood gives us.

The institutional church, however, is an organization. And as much as I love our Assemblies of God denomination, I also know that the more institutionalized it becomes, the more paralyzed it will be in expressing the life of Christ on earth. There are three things that I fear, and I've mentioned them before when speaking to this group. They are: the institutionalization of the church, the professionalization of the ministry, and the intellectualization of the Pentecostal experience.

I pray for the day when people will again be baptized in the Holy Spirit at the altars of our churches; not at women's conventions, not at men's conventions, not at Royal Rangers Pow-Wows, and not at youth camps. Why must we parcel this experience out? It needs to be happening in our churches. I do think there are signs that an increasing number of churches are beginning to realize this. People *are* beginning to be filled with the Holy Spirit once again at our altars.

### One Body . . . many members

We are members of His Body. His blood gives us life. As much as I respect our General Superintendent as the head of the Assemblies of God, the only living link I have with him is through the blood of Jesus Christ. This blood that links me to him also links me to all other believers, not just Assemblies of God believers. The provincialism or denominational ethnocentrism so prevalent today ignores the fact that God has many, many, many children outside the Assemblies of God. We are a very small part of His family.

As we take Communion today, we need to examine how we really feel about our brothers and sisters who are not of the Assemblies of God. Do we see them as distant cousins or God's stepchildren? Or are they—with us—members of His Body Whose blood gives us all eternal life? When we are converted and baptized, we become members of the Body of Christ, not of the Assemblies of God. We are, in an awesome sense, far more responsible to the head of that Body than we are to our denominational leaders. And we are responsible not only to the Head but to every other member of the Body.

The way I behave as an Assemblies of God Christian also affects what people think of Baptist Christians and Methodist Christians and Church of Christ Christians. It affects what people think of members of the family of God in every other denomination. My behavior elevates them in public opinion, or embarrasses them in public opinion.

We need to examine ourselves this morning as to how we feel about members of the Body of Christ who are not members of the Assemblies of God. For, as members of Christ's Body, we need each other. It's easy to become so engrossed in the work we are doing, and so convinced of its extreme importance, that we neglect others who are *just as called* to do other work. Or, worse yet, we criticize them. If the Church is to be a healthy Body, we need every member and we need those members doing the work they have been called to do for Jesus Christ.

When we foster individualism and isolationism in the Body of Christ, we hinder and destroy the work of Christ. As members of His Body, we need mutual respect for each other. When any limb or organ of the physical body fails to function properly, the whole body is affected. When I catch my thumb in the door, I don't say, "My thumb has a pain." Oh, no, friends. When that happens, my whole body has a pain! Its epicenter may be in my thumb, but my whole body feels it. That's the sense God wants us to have as we approach Communion, that we are members of one another and when one of us hurts, all of us are in pain.

### Examining who we are becoming

Members of the Body of Christ are to serve one another. Paul makes this very clear in 1 Corinthians 12. It's so easy *not* to be servant-minded; to foster a spirit of elitism instead. But that cripples the Body of Christ. We should never bestow the kind of adulation on anyone that encourages that kind of mindset. As a denomination, we should have learned that in the '80s; but, with every revival, there comes an elevation of the personalities most directly connected with it. There comes the temptation within the Body to bestow a kind of elitist hero worship on the revival leaders. This is destructive for them personally and for the Body as a whole.

I probably don't need to remind you how embarrassed the whole Body of Christ was when so many prominent ministers experienced moral failure in the 1980s. But those events could have been predicted by the elitism and hero status this denomination had bestowed on those brothers for *years* before those tragic events occurred.

We should not only refuse to bestow that elitism on others; we should refuse to accept it for ourselves. I had ministered in the churches and organizations run by those brothers who got into trouble in the '80s. It was an unusual atmosphere at times. People offered to carry my Bible, to open doors for me, and even to massage my feet! And, friends, neither my spirit nor any other human spirit is sanctified enough to accept that kind of elitist treatment without seeing it give birth to spiritual pride and conceit in his or her heart.

I don't know whether I'm speaking prophetically here or not; the future will tell, but I am asking you as a body to do something I believe is very important. We must apply *the same standards of accountability to which we are held* to those who are prominent leaders of revival movements. They need those lines drawn for them, and we must have the courage to do that.

Otherwise, the first thing you know, someone of great prominence will come into your community to minister—without an invitation on the part of your denomination—and you will be forced to either cooperate or appear to oppose someone that many believe is *God's servant for this hour*. If you allow that to happen, you deserve the consequences you will face, for this is the bestowing of an elitism that eventually destroys those who are foolish enough to accept it and victimizes those who are foolish enough to give it.

### A spirit of "elitism" cripples the Body of Christ

I carry my own Bible. I open my own doors. I put on my own pants—one leg at a time. And we should require that of anyone who serves the Lord, regardless of the eminence of his or her gifts. Fostering a spirit of elitism will eventually cripple and bring humiliation to the Body of Christ. We shouldn't bestow this kind of "ministry superstar" status *on* others, and we shouldn't accept it *from* others.

This morning, as we approach the Table of the Lord, we need to examine ourselves . . . our personal relationship with Christ, our relationships with others in our local body of believers, and our relationship to the entire Body of Christ universal—what some people would call the Holy Catholic Church. The word "Catholic" simply means "universal." And we are part of God's Holy Catholic or universal—and united—Church.

In Ephesians 4:4-6, Paul exhorts the early believers to unity based on oneness of the Body: one Body, one Spirit, one Lord, one faith, one baptism, and one God and Father of all. In that passage, he charges the church leaders with keeping the Body of Christ united. That's still our job. Unity in the Body of Christ is damaged by mistrust, anger, unwholesome talk, bitterness, wrath, and clamor—there are a number of these damaging attitudes and behaviors catalogued for us in Ephesians 4:25-31. None of them should be a part of the believer's life.

Following Paul's inspired instructions and allowing our character to be shaped by them will help bring the Church into unity. As each of us approaches the Lord's Table today, let us examine ourselves and put aside those thoughts and feelings that would divide us. Let us focus on His Body and Blood—the price He paid to unite us—so that each of us may experience the grace of His forgiveness, in turn forgiving others as God for Christ's sake has forgiven us.

---

[1] 2 Corinthians 5:8.
[2] Acts 26:8, NIV.
[3] Revelation 13:8.
[4] Acts 8:3, 1 Corinthians 15:9, Galatians 1:13.
[5] R.H. McDaniel, 20th Century, © (renewal) 1942, Rodeheaver Company.
[6] Romans 8:1-4.

# 14

# Winning the Battle for Your Heart *

Let me take this opportunity to thank all of those who so faithfully remembered Priscilla and me in your prayers over the past several months. This time last year, I had no idea what I would soon be facing. Thank God, we're now about eight months beyond my heart surgery and I am enjoying His gift of good health once again. The earthly "tent" in which I live has been expertly *mended* by the best surgical team we could find . . . but we know that it has been *healed* by the God Who created it and we thank Him every day for the gift He has given us.

This morning, as I looked at the photographs of fellow ministers who have gone to be with the Lord since our last District Council meeting, I thought of how close I had come to also leaving behind my own earthly tent.[1] God let me know that He still has some things for me to accomplish here on earth, and so I am here with you today.

I also thought, as I looked at those photographs, of a television news program I recently saw about a young woman who had disappeared from her family more than 30 years ago. In a community far away from her home, someone a short time ago found the body of a young woman wrapped up in tent canvas. She didn't match the description of any person missing from the local area, and the community eventually buried her with a great deal of honor as the "tent lady." That was the name on her tombstone.

Criminal investigators in the hometown of the woman who had been missing for over 30 years heard the story and got legal permission

---

* Sermon for the Communion Service of the 1998 Ohio District Council of the Asssemblies of God, Christian Life Center, Dayton, Ohio.

to exhume the body for examination, in case it might be their missing person. The news cameras showed all that was left of the funeral shroud; just a small piece of a veil. Of course there was no flesh and no identifiable body—just bones. They crushed a bone segment into powder and subjected it to modern techniques of DNA identification. From this they were able to tell that family many miles away that their daughter's body had at last been located. She was the "tent lady." And the tent lady had a name, at last.

Well, you and I are also wrapped up in a tent called skin. And one of these days, just as our brothers and sisters in the Lord have done before us, we will find our earthly tent has been folded. Our remains will be laid to rest as we begin to enjoy eternity with our Lord and Savior—the creator of that unique DNA code that helped those earthly investigators identify the tent lady! But, friends, Jesus won't need a DNA code to identify us; He knows us by name. In fact, He knew us before we ever took our first breath of earth's air! How's that for identification? And He's prepared a home for us that will be ready upon our arrival. Aren't you glad you serve such a God?

I want to thank the musicians this morning for giving us an opportunity to pause and reflect. For a period of several years, we seemed to have lost our ability to celebrate in worship. Well, the recent revival spirit has helped us rediscover our ability to celebrate. However, along with the celebration, we need to provide time during our worship services to quietly reflect on the goodness of God in an attitude that allows Him opportunity to speak to us. You've done that here this morning and I just want to express my appreciation for your openness to this part of the worship experience. In the joy of our celebration, we do not want to lose the sense of awe and wonder we feel when we quietly enter into God's presence and hear Him speak to our hearts.

Well, let's get to our text this morning. We're going to be reading from several locations; first, Proverbs 23:7: " . . . *For as he thinketh in his heart, so is he.*"

Now let's turn to Matthew 15:17-20:

> *"Do not ye yet understand, that whatsoever entereth in at the mouth goeth into the belly, and is cast out into the draught? But those things which proceed out of the mouth come forth*

*from the heart; and they defile the man. For out of the heart proceed evil thoughts, murders, adulteries, fornications, thefts, false witness, blasphemies. These are the things which defile a man: but to eat with unwashen hands defileth not a man."*

Now let's go to Matthew 12:34,35, where Jesus says:

*" . . . For out of the abundance of the heart the mouth speaketh. A good man out of the good treasure of the heart bringeth forth good things: and an evil man out of the evil treasure bringeth forth evil things."*

Then, let's look at Psalm 139:23 and Psalm 19:14:

*"Search me, O God, and know my heart: try me, and know my thoughts: And see if there be any wicked way in me, and lead me in the way everlasting."* And, *"Let the words of my mouth, and the meditation of my heart, be acceptable in thy sight, O Lord, my strength, and my redeemer."*

Shall we bow our hearts in prayer.

*Lord, we're so often concerned about what others see in us. Make us more concerned about what You see in us. We pray this morning that You'll help us see the wisdom of caring more about what You see and less about what others see in our lives. For we know that when we open our inner being to You, You will help us weed out those potential behaviors which would embarrass us, disgrace Your kingdom, and be a stumbling block to many who look to us for leadership.*

*Help us to see that greatness in Your sight begins with purity of heart and transparency before You, not with man-made greatness. Make us aware that there's a supernatural war being waged for our hearts, and teach us how to be triumphant in that battle. Anoint us this morning with Your Holy Spirit so that what You want to be said will be said and what You want to be heard will be heard. And now we commit ourselves to You in Jesus' Name, Amen.*

Occasionally, as I view the skyline of a great metroplex out the window of an airplane, I remind myself that long before construction teams raised any of those skyscrapers from the dust, every one of them existed in the heart and mind of its architect. What a tribute to the creative genius of human beings! And how easy it is to *take for granted* or even *abuse* this power that God has invested in us.

On other occasions, traveling to and from the airports of those same cities, I pass through the seamy and shameful areas of town and remind myself that the same human creative genius that can build skyscrapers is also responsible for the debauchery of our cities. The human heart and mind have an awesome capacity for good and evil. Your heart and mind are always active, even when you sleep. And the activity of the human mind is far more than the product of nutrition and neurochemical interaction: it is the battleground for intense spiritual warfare.

The battle for your heart is waged in your mind. The battle for my heart is waged in my mind. Our mental activity is spirit-driven. Let me say that again: mental activity is spirit-driven. If you want to have some control over the content of your heart in the future, you must be extremely aware of the invisible activity of your mental processes. The *visible* reality of your history comes out of the *invisible* activity of your mental processes. The fantasies of your heart today are highly likely to become the realities of your life tomorrow.

This is what Jesus is teaching us in the two passages we read from Matthew. What we accumulate in our hearts will eventually determine our conversation and our behavior. The visible activities of our lives flow out of the invisible activities of our heart. Have you recently tuned in to your heart and listened to your thoughts? I think this is one of the reasons why the apostle admonishes us to *"Study to be quiet."*[2]

What have you found yourself saying to yourself lately? For, the most important conversation of your life is not one you have with another human being; rather, it is the conversation you have with yourself. And that self-conversation proceeds at a speed of approximately 3,000 to 4,000 words per minute—about ten times the rate of actual speech when we are talking with another person.

### Keeping "body and soul" together in church

The easiest, simplest part of coming to church is bringing your *body* here. The most difficult part of coming to church is keeping your *mind* here. We learn this skill of separating mind from body very early in life. All parents soon discover that although they may be able to force us as children to put our bodies in certain places, they can't force us to keep our little minds there. So, I ask you again, have you tuned in to the conversations you are having with yourself lately?

Your thought life is the seedbed from which your future grows. It's a short distance between the imaginations of your life today and the facts of your life tomorrow. And temptation begins in your imagination.

This morning, I hope to engage in some preventive maintenance. Since 1988, we have seen over 1,500 ministers and missionaries at EMERGE. Most of them have simply gotten burned out in the work of the Lord. But far too many of them have gone to sleep to what's happening in the hidden world of their urges, fantasies, and ideas. So, by the time we see them, their behavior has embarrassed them, disgraced the Kingdom, and become a stumbling block to the very cause of Christ they had committed themselves to promoting.

Temptation doesn't begin at the scene of the fall. Temptation begins in your imagination long before you reach that scene. Every person who falls into temptation has first had to be defeated in his or her imaginations. God's Word declares, *"For as he [or she] thinketh in his [or her] heart, so is he [or she]."*[3] In other words, the habits of your life are first the habits of your heart and mind.

William Shakespeare ironically put many words of wisdom in the mouth of a character named Polonius, whom critics describe as, "a windy fool . . . a lovable windbag who [misunderstood] almost everything."[4] Among Polonius' gems is this:

> *"This above all—to thine own self be true,*
> *And it must follow, as the night the day,*
> *Thou canst not then be false to any man."*[5]

Both God and Satan know that temptation begins in our imaginations. And both God and Satan are battling for our imaginations because they know that whoever wins that battle will have their presence expressed through our bodies. This is the uniqueness of the human body, that it can transform *spiritual impression* into *physical expression.*

**The seeds of behavior are sown in the mind**

The one thing that makes our bodies different from the bodies of any other creatures God ever made is that the seeds of our behavior are sown in the invisible activity of our mind. We are capable of giving physical expression to the invisible spirit being who wins the battle for our choices. In fact, we are *in*capable of *not giving physical expression* to the invisible spirit who wins the battle for our choices. That's why that battle rages for as long as we live. And the battle begins in our imagination.

This is seen as far back as the Garden of Eden. From the presence of Satan, the power of sin-stimulated urges, fantasies, and ideas of disobedience came into the fantasy life of Eden's pair. I've operationally defined sin this way:

*SIN is an invisible power that emanates from Satan. It impacts on the mind to stimulate the brain to think in terms of urges, fantasies, and ideas that detract from and destroy one's divine potential.*

Every activity that we display comes from one or a combination of these sources: urges, fantasies, or ideas. Sometimes, long after the fact when I'm trying to help people rebuild their lives, I will ask them how they explain this action to themselves. Often, I hear them say, "I don't know. I just had an urge to do it. The idea just came into my mind. I couldn't get the picture out of my mind."

That's where it all begins. With an urge. With a fantasy. With an idea. And out of that invisible conglomeration of urges, fantasies, and ideas, behavior and attitude come.

It was Eve's imagination that got her into trouble. When she looked at the fruit of the tree and knew that it was desired to make one wise, she was well on her way to falling victim to Satan. It wasn't the *sight* of the tree, but it was the *imagination* that the tree excited in Eve that caused her to fall. She looked at that tree and saw it as a way to become like God. She imagined; she fantasized; she ate.

Now, ladies, don't let your husbands make you feel guilty for being daughters of Eve. Remind them it took a *devil* to tempt a woman . . . but it only took a *woman* to tempt a man.

By the time of Noah, the Holy Spirit says that , except for Noah, *" . . . every imagination of the thoughts of [a man's] heart was only evil continually."*[6] That's an awesome statement. The thought life—the mental activity of the entire human race, except for Noah—had degenerated in these few centuries to the place where the Holy Spirit says the imaginations of men's hearts were only, and continually evil.

The well-watered plains of Jordan revealed more to Lot than healthy vegetation. As he looked at the fertile plain, he saw that it would give him the competitive edge he needed to become richer and more powerful than his uncle. And even though competition is very American, it is not biblical. The whole aim of competition is to make a winner out of me . . . and a loser out of you. The whole aim of competition can be summed up in the game of "one-upmanship."

**The only godly competition is with ourself.**

*"So fight I not as one that beateth the air: but I keep under my body and bring it into subjection, lest that by any means, when I have preached to others, I myself should be a castaway."*[7] It wasn't Lot's appreciation of healthy vegetation that took him into the well-watered plains of Sodom and Gomorrah. It was his selfish desire to exceed the wealth and prosperity of Abraham that took him there.

Look at what a little creative imagination prompted Rebecca and Jacob to do to old, blind, Isaac. They dreamed up a way to make goat meat taste like venison. They imagined a scheme that could make a plain, smooth-skinned man like Jacob feel like his hairy brother, Esau. Where did that genius come from? The enemy impacted the mind to stimulate the brain to think in terms of urges, fantasies, and ideas . . . . He is very, very subtle and very, very persuasive.

What about David's scheme to get Bathsheba? Seeing how desirable she was and knowing that he could not lawfully or morally have her, David's imagination concocted an ingenious plan for committing adultery with her. He exercised his power as king to bring Bathsheba to his bed. After all, what desire of the king should be denied him? Positions of power can be very, very dangerous.

All of us know the horror of the 80s when heroes and champions in the church fell one after another. There has to be a lot of arrogance associated with that. After all, these are people who were reaching thousands and tens of thousands. And I'm sure, when drawn away and enticed, they—like every other person who falls—went through religious rituals: "Cleanse me with Your blood, Lord Jesus." Then they probably spoke in tongues to reassure themselves that the Spirit of God had not departed from them. Then they could return to the platform to preach more energetically, to prove that they still had the anointing. And when people were saved and healed, the enemy used those signs that followed the preaching of God's Word to bury these men in their own self-deception.

It is so easy to conclude that the results of preaching indicate that God is continuing to bless a preacher's blatantly flawed life. But remember, friends, *God will honor His Word even if the devil preaches.* Results from our preaching are never a vindication of our lives; they are a vindication of God's Word.

When David knew that Bathsheba was pregnant by him, he tried to persuade her husband to come home from battle and lay with her so the pregnancy could be attributed to him. But Uriah had chosen to take a high moral road of loyalty to his comrades in arms; a road that would not be rewarded by the king. Uriah's highly moral behavior cost him his life. Those who take the high road are often not rewarded in this life. Remember what God's Word tells us: *"If in this life only we have hope in Christ, we are of all [people] most miserable."*[8]

As David lay awake at night, looking for a solution to his dilemma, Satan invaded his fantasies and helped him concoct a scheme that would cover up the evidence of his own lust by having Uriah killed in battle. David simply gave instructions to Joab, his general, to send Uriah where the fighting was most fierce. Then Joab was ordered to withdraw support troops so that Uriah would be killed and Bathsheba could be David's.

Then there was Judas. He thought he'd covered all the bases to make it possible for him to stay within the inner circle of the Lord and still enjoy his thirty extra pieces of silver.

And remember the brainstorm that backfired on Ananiah and Sapphira. People in the church who were giving sacrificially were finding places of honor among the saints. Wanting that honor without the cost,

Satan put it in the hearts and minds of this couple to lie to the Holy Spirit.

## We are all flawed and fallen

And so I ask us, this morning, what have our thoughts been saying to us lately? Don't underestimate their influence. For, the fantasies of your life today may indeed become the facts of your life tomorrow. No carnal weapons can wipe our fantasies free from these kinds of temptations. And none of us is above them, for we are all flawed and fallen.

This reminds me of the story of an old seminarian who was walking down the street with one of his graduate students when a young woman, obviously blessed of God, passed by on the other side. And the young man just found himself automatically following her with his eyes when he became aware of who he was with. Abruptly, he caught himself and said to the old professor, "Oh, sir, I'll be so glad when I get old enough where things like that won't bother me."

And the wise old seminary professor mused, "And so will I, son. So will I."

We are all flawed and fallen. Paul warns us in 1 Corinthians 10:12, *"Wherefore let him that thinketh he standeth take heed lest he fall."* For the enemy is far wiser than you and me. And long before he seeks to chronicle his deeds in the history of your life and mine, he plants his thoughts in our imaginations. Is it any wonder that David prayed, *"Let the words of my mouth, and the meditation of my heart, be acceptable in thy sight, O Lord, my strength, and my redeemer."*[9]

Please don't misunderstand me. I do not believe that when we stand at the Judgment Seat of Christ we will be judged for our thoughts. For the Scriptures plainly teach us that we, *" . . . must all appear before the judgment seat of Christ, that each one may receive what is due him for the things done while in the body, whether good or bad."*[10] But if you are tempted to think you can play around with your thoughts and not eventually have those thoughts become deeds, then you are ignoring the warning Jesus gives us when He says, if you don't want to commit the act of adultery, you don't indulge in adulterous thoughts (Matthew 5:28).

*"Search me, O God, and know my heart; try me and know my thoughts. And see if there be any wicked way in me, and lead me in the way everlasting."*[11] David knew well where the enemy strikes first. He understood the destructive power of sinful imaginations to explode in one's mind and heart until the deeds of his life shatter his character and destroy his future. Although it is recorded that God called David *"a man after mine own heart,"*[12] being that kind of man did not protect David from the bitterness of the loss of a child. That loss would be a lifelong memory of carelessness in his thought life.

Remember, the enemy will take you farther than you want to go, keep you longer than you want to stay, and charge you more than you want to pay. Then, when he has you hooked on his pleasure, he will flash the price tag. And the pleasure is never worth the price.

### Faith also begins in our imagination

Imagination is the seedbed from which faith in God begins to sprout and grow. The same imagination and fantasy that provides a seedbed for temptation is also capable of becoming a source of triumphant faith in Christ.

I have already given you my operational definition of sin. I've operationally defined eternal life also. This is the power that many believers aren't even aware they possess. Sometime, when you want a little amusement at a church gathering, ask people who are familiar with the term to explain to you what "eternal life" is. You'll be amazed at how few people can tell you what eternal life really is. Most of them will say it's what is going to keep them alive after they're dead. Well . . . until you die, of what practical benefit is it for you to have it? Others will say that eternal life is what's going to take them "up" when Jesus comes. But what about the time until He comes? How does eternal life make you any different from your pagan neighbor? Can you identify eternal life by the urges, fantasies, and ideas it stimulates in your mind? With that thought, let's consider this operational definition of "eternal life:"

*ETERNAL LIFE is an invisible power to which the unregenerate are insensitive. It emanates from—it comes right out of—the Person of Christ. It impacts on the mind of the regenerate person to stimulate the brain to think in terms of urges, fantasies, and ideas that enhance and develop our divine potential.*

The sad fact is that until you are born again, you are incapable of responding to eternal life. That part of you is *"dead in trespasses and sin."*[13] And that's the part of us that's regenerated when Christ brings us to life: it's the ability to hear His voice in our urges, our fantasies, and our ideas.

God's will for your tomorrow is found in your imagination today. For example, no one had seen an ark before Noah built one. How did he do that? God gave him the plans. Where? In his imagination.

Abraham had no idea where the "Promised Land" was when he began his journey, but he got there—and his wife was full of faith for following him. How did Abraham get there? The Lord showed him where it was.

Moses had never seen anything like the Tabernacle. But when he finished it, God found it so completely to His liking that He moved in and stayed for forty years.

Even in the midst of a degenerate people of *"unclean lips,"*[14] Isaiah saw the Lord. Where did he see Him? Isaiah saw Him in the imagination of his mind: the Lord was *"high and lifted up, and his train filled the temple."*[15] And Isaiah heard the Lord say, *"Whom shall I send? And who will go for us?"*[16] All of this happened in Isaiah's mind.

From this, God wants us to understand that regardless of how wicked the people around us may be, their evil cannot keep us from seeing the Lord and hearing His will for our life if our hearts are fixed on Him. Look at what God was able to show Daniel: a whole span of history and prophecy was spread before him. He saw it in his mind centuries before it ever came to pass.

Because Peter's imagination was at the Lord's disposal on a housetop one day, God was able to transform his life while he was in a trance. What Peter saw and heard that day cured him of his prejudices (Acts 10:1-43). And I think that's the real test of the spiritual source of any presumed manifestation of the Spirit. Regardless of the manifestation, its validity is found in the fruit it produces. And if the manifestation doesn't produce the fruit, then we have to question its origin and wonder how much of it is self-seeking and attention-getting behavior. For the purpose of the manifestation of the Spirit of God is to increase and multiply the fruit of the Spirit in our lives.

Peter's life and mind were so transformed that day, his thinking was so changed, that God could use his preaching not only to open the kingdom of God to the Jews on the Day of Pentecost, but also to open the kingdom of God to the Gentiles at the home of Cornelius. If we will learn to recognize God in the mental processes of our mind, He will make us so flexible that we will be amazed by the variety of circumstances in which He can use us.

We deal with a lot of religious rigidity at EMERGE. We have a scale on the MMPI-2 test (Minnesota Multiphasic Personality Inventory/ 2) called the "lie scale." Religious people tend to score high on it, and preachers and missionary candidates tend to score the highest of all. The "lie scale" includes such statements as . . .

*I read all the editorials in the newspaper.* And they answer "YES."

*I seldom vote for anybody I don't know about.* "YES."

*My manners are just as good when I'm eating by myself as they are when I'm eating in a fine restaurant.* "YES."

We are so fearful of what other people will think of us! The most dangerous place in the world to be transparent is at church. Why? Because people at church are pretending to be what they're not, and it's hard to be honest around people who are pretending to be perfect.

Rigidity will *restrict* the places and ways God can use you. Flexibility will *increase* the places and the ways God can use you. Perhaps there was never a person in the history of Christianity any more rigid than Saul of Tarsus. But after being worked over by the Holy Spirit for three years in Arabia, that rigidity was transformed into amazing flexibility. In his letter to the Corinthian church, Paul wrote, *"To the weak became I as weak that I might gain the weak; I am made all things to all men, that I might by all means save some."*[17]

While John was in the Spirit on the Lord's Day, his imagination was overwhelmed with what he saw and heard, as God trusted him with the Revelation of Jesus Christ.

### The real "holy war" takes place in your mind

In your heart and mine, there is an awesome capacity for good and evil. God and the devil are waging a holy war to see whose stimulation will find expression in your body and mind. And you can tell how the battle is going by tuning in to your heart. When nobody is around, or when you shut out everyone who is around, what have your thoughts been saying to you lately?

Has Satan been able to take advantage of that awesome faculty of your imagination to accuse you? To torment you? To threaten you? To defeat you? To make you feel unappreciated or more persecuted than your brothers or sisters? Or have you waited before God and truly had an " . . . *ear to hear what the Spirit saith unto the churches*"?[18] There, in that tremendously creative, uniquely human faculty of the heart, allow God to bring to life His plan and His purpose so that your fantasies become the seedbed from which faith springs to give you victory in your life with Christ.

Are you able to stop destructive fantasies from deluging your mind with their message of doom and despair? Well, the Bible says that the child of God has weapons that are *"(not carnal, but mighty through God to the pulling down of strong holds;) Casting down imaginations, and every high thing that exalteth itself against the knowledge of God."*[19] These are the weapons that can help me bring my thoughts into captivity to the Lordship of Christ.

Paul said, *"My earnest expectation and my hope . . ."* is that *"Christ shall be magnified in my body, whether it be by life, or by death . . . ."*[20] Your body is all of you that I can see; I can't see your heart. But if He's alive there in your heart, people need to see that reflected in your body.

My biggest enemy is not outside of me. My biggest enemy is inside of me. And I must be aware of how he stimulates me to think; how he tempts me to feel; how he urges me to speak and act. Why? Because my body is uniquely created by God to reflect, in my speech, attitudes, and behavior, the one who wins the battle for my heart through my mental activity. I need God's help in bringing into captivity every thought that goes through my mind to the obedience of Christ.

Every night, whether we're together at home or on the road, Priscilla and I pray a "Prayer of Honesty" that I've adapted from Lutheran liturgy. My adaptation goes something like this:

*"Oh, merciful Father, I confess that I am in bondage to sin and I cannot free myself. For I have sinned against You in thought and word and deed...."* Notice the progression—sin goes from thought, to word, to deed: *"... By the things that I have done."* There aren't as many of those now as there used to be, but there are still enough to condemn me. And even when I clean up those things that I should not have done, but did, there are still those things I should have done—but didn't. *"I have sinned against You in thought and word and deed by the things which I have done and by the things which I have left undone. For I have not loved You with my whole heart."*

I'm glad to see the intensity of our hunger and zeal for God today. But He still has just a very little part of us. I've been saved and filled with the Spirit for 55 years, ever since I was 15 years of age. And I'm close enough to the end of the journey now to wonder what will happen when I stand at the Judgment Seat of Christ and the fire of that day reduces my life to its eternal residue. How many of those 55 years will He Who knows me best see that I have served Him with my whole heart; loved Him with my whole heart?

Notice how quiet it's getting here. My friend Martha Tennyson would say that people don't talk much when they're in surgery. I hope the Lord will be able to find a few days, perhaps a few weeks or months (and I wouldn't be more ambitious than that), when I've loved Him with my whole heart. *"I've not loved You with my whole heart. I've not loved my neighbor as myself."*

### Thou shalt love thy neighbor as thyself

We get so excited about all of our institutional idiosyncrasies; should we baptize once backward or three times face-forward? Should we sprinkle or immerse? Should we do it in the Name of the Father, Son, and Holy Ghost, or should we do it in Jesus' Name? We get so caught up with all of the tag-on baggage that we fail to judge ourselves by the big two commandments: *"Thou shalt love the Lord thy God with all thy heart, and with all thy soul, and with all thy mind . . . Thou shalt love thy neighbor as thyself."*[21]

Think of the years we lost worrying about the length of a person's hair! For awhile we were worried because women wore it too short; then we got worried because men wore it too long. But the two big things that worry me are that I have not loved God with my whole heart and I have not loved my neighbor as myself.

And here's the conclusion of that Prayer of Honesty: *"For the sake of your Son, Jesus Christ, have mercy on me. Forgive me. Cleanse me. And renew me, that I may walk in Thy way and delight in Thy will, to the glory of Thy holy Name."*

What are the weapons He gives us to fight with? The first is praise. *"Enter into his gates with thanksgiving, and into his courts with praise."*[22] When you're downhearted, when you're discouraged, when you're entering into the throes of depression, try praising the Lord. Paul and Silas, with their feet held fast in the stocks, found the way to deal with their circumstance was in giving praise to God at midnight.

### Learn to filter your thoughts

The second weapon is prayer, and not just what we say on our knees. We need to practice the discipline of monitoring our thoughts and letting God's Word, committed to memory, help us discern which of our thoughts are coming from Him and which are coming from His enemy. This is praying without ceasing. In computer terms, it's making the written Word of God the operating system of your life and the living Word of God the power that turns on your hard drive.

This is how we begin to filter through Scripture what we feel in our urges, what we see in our fantasies, and what we think in our thoughts. And only the Word of God can be trusted with that responsibility: *"Thy word is a lamp unto my feet, and a light unto my path."*[23] *"Thy Word have I hid in mine heart, that I might not sin against thee."*[24] *"For the Word of God is quick, and powerful, and sharper than any two-edged sword."*[25] And when it's finished with its work in us, it becomes a discerner of the thoughts and intents of our heart.[26]

And what about the provision of the atonement? *"And they overcame him by the blood of the Lamb, and by the word of their testimony."*[27] When the devil reminds you of your past, remind him of his future. Overcome him through the blood of the Lamb.

Remember the power of the Spirit. When the enemy comes in like a flood, the Spirit of the Lord raises up a standard against him. In ancient times, a *standard* was the banner that the king or his highest military representative carried in the front lines of battle, leading the charge against an enemy. The standard-bearer let the rest of the soldiers know where the lines of the battle were at any given moment.

### Stay behind the standard-bearer!

Soldiers *followed* the standard—they didn't get out in front of it. And the Holy Spirit of God raises up a *spiritual standard* against the enemy of our souls, leading the charge against him. Our job is *to follow* His leading—*not to lead* the fight. We're no match for Satan in our own strength. The standard-bearer goes before us.

I deal with a lot of Christians who try to produce the fruit of the Spirit in the energy of the flesh. Their faith is sort of like the first part of the Boy Scouts' pledge: "On my honor, I will do my best to do my duty to God and my country." These believers have a "manual" they seek to obey by sheer will power—but that's a tough way to serve the Lord. None of us can produce the fruit of the Spirit in the energy of the flesh.

Several months ago I was helping a man deal with pornography. When I explained to him the operational definitions of sin and eternal life I shared with you, he began to make the connection between which of his urges and thoughts and ideas were coming from whom. He said, "This is the first time in my life that I have ever felt I had access to an ally in getting this monkey off my back. Every other time I've attempted it, I've done so only through the sheer power of my will."

Now, please don't misunderstand me. Our will is involved. But it can't be our only power source in this battle. Can you imagine what a time we'd have getting out on the highway today if we had to steer our automobiles without our power steering? Could you turn the wheel? No. Nor could I. No one among us could turn that steering wheel alone if the power supply was cut off. It's been a long time since I felt what I would feel if I tried to steer a car by my own power. But when the power steering is working—when the power source is connected—we can turn that steering wheel with one little finger.

Walking in the Spirit is not difficult. It's simply acknowledging that without the power of One who is greater than he that is in the world,[28] I can't take this body where it needs to go. I can't cause these lips to say what they need to say. And I can't make this brain do what it needs to do. I can only do those things in the power of the Spirit.

Throughout the day, every day, ask God frequently to help you discern the spiritual origin of your imaginations so that the facts of your future will reflect the triumph of your faith and not the tragedy of your temptations. For, your heart is the spiritual seedbed of your future. The tragedies or triumphs of your tomorrows are growing there today. *"Search me, O God, and know my heart: try me, and know my thoughts. And see if there be any wicked way in me, and lead me in the way everlasting."*[29] *"Let the words of my mouth, and the meditation of my heart, be acceptable in thy sight, O Lord, my strength, and my redeemer."*[30]

Shall we pray.

---

[1] 2 Corinthians 5:1, NASB.
[2] 1 Thessalonians 4:11.
[3] Proverbs 23:7.
[4] Davis, J. Madison and Frankforter, A. Daniel **The Shakespeare Name Dictionary**. New York: Garland Publishers, 1995, p. 391-2.
[5] Shakespeare, William. **The Tragedy of Hamlet, Prince of Denmark**, Act 1, Scene 3, lines 78-80.
[6] Genesis 6:5.
[7] 1 Corinthians 9:26,27.
[8] 1 Corinthians 15:19.
[9] Psalm 19:14.
[10] 2 Corinthians 5:10, NIV.
[11] Psalm 139:23,24.
[12] Acts 13:22.
[13] Ephesians 2:1.
[14] Isaiah 6:5.
[15] Isaiah 6:1.
[16] Isaiah 6:8.
[17] 1 Corinthians 9:22.

[18] Revelation 2:7.
[19] 2 Corinthians 10:4,5.
[20] Philippians 1:20,21.
[21] Matthew 22:37,39.
[22] Psalm 100:4.
[23] Psalm 119:105.
[24] Psalm 119:11.
[25] Hebrews 4:12.
[26] Ibid.
[27] Revelation 12:11.
[28] 1 John 4:4.
[29] Psalm 139:23,24.
[30] Psalm 19:14.

# 15
## Judged or Justified? *

*"Therefore thou art inexcusable, O man, whosoever thou art that judgest: for wherein thou judgest another, thou condemnest thyself' for thou that judgest does the same things. But we are sure that the judgment of God is according to truth against them which commit such things. And thinkest thou this, O man, that judgest them which do such things, and doest the same, that thou shalt escape the judgment of God? Or despisest thou the riches of his goodness and forbearance and longsuffering; not knowing that the goodness of God leadeth thee to repentance?*

*"But after thy hardness and impenitent heart treasurest up unto thyself wrath against the day of wrath and revelation of the righteous judgment of God; Who will render to every man according to his deeds; To them who by patient continuance in well-doing seek for glory and honour and immortality, eternal life; But unto them that are contentious, and do not obey the truth, but obey unrighteousness, indignation and wrath, Tribulation and anguish, upon every soul of man that doeth evil, of the Jew first, and also of the Gentile;*

*"But glory, honour, and peace, to every man that worketh good, to the Jew first, and also to the Gentile: For there is no respect of persons with God. For as many as have sinned*

---

* Sermon for the Communion Service of the 1999 Ohio District Council of the Assemblies of God, Bethel Temple, Parma, Ohio.

*without law shall also perish without law: and as many as have sinned in the law shall be judged by the law;*

*"(For not the hearers of the law are just before God, but the doers of the law shall be justified. For when the Gentiles, which have not the law, do by nature the things contained in the law, these, having not the law, are a law unto themselves: Which shew the work of the law written in their hearts, their conscience also bearing witness, and their thoughts the mean while* accusing or else excusing one another;)

*"In the day when God shall judge the secrets of men by Jesus Christ according to my gospel."*[1]

*"If we have forgotten the name of our God, or stretched out our hands to a strange god, Shall not God search this out? For he knoweth the secrets of the heart."*[2]

*"For as often as ye eat this bread, and drink this cup, ye do shew the Lord's death till he come. Wherefore whosoever shall eat this bread, and drink this cup of the Lord, unworthily, shall be guilty of the body and blood of the Lord. But let a man examine himself, and so let him eat of that bread, and drink of that cup.*

*"For he that eateth and drinketh unworthily, eateth and drinketh damnation to himself, not discerning the Lord's body. For this cause many are weak and sickly among you, and many sleep.*

*"For if we would judge ourselves, we should not be judged. But when we are judged, we are chastened of the Lord, that we should not be condemned with the world."*[3]

*"Therefore being justified by faith, we have peace with God through our Lord Jesus Christ."*[4]

This Council brings to an end my work as the Assistant Superintendent of the Ohio District Council. Putting closure on certain phases of your life when they are over is very important to your spiritual and emotional health.

So, I have spent several months anticipating this moment and preparing myself for it. After all, you can't move ahead into the next room of your life to effectively tend to the tasks waiting for you there if you haven't closed the door to the room of life you are leaving. And you can't hang around a half-closed door for long . . . or you'll find your hand getting caught as someone else tries to close that door *for you.*

### Learn to put closure on the past

Some of the saddest people I have met, personally or professionally, are those who have not been able to put closure on the past. They see little hope in the future. They have little or no joy in the present. Often they are angry, depressed, self-pitying people because they refuse to deal with the past and get on with life.

Part of bringing closure on whatever task you have finished is realizing that however you have done it is the way it must be left. Nothing is to be gained by reliving the past and wishing you had done things differently. When the past was the present, each of us had the opportunity to make what appeared to us at the time to be the best and wisest choices. Second-guessing yourself is not a very healthy way to spend the rest of your life. You are not likely to get where you want to be in the future by continually looking over your shoulder at the past.

It is rather sobering to know that I can never do anything to improve my record of service to the Lord, our District Superintendents, our Executive Presbytery, our District Presbytery Board, or you who have given me this honor for 30 years. I'm sure I have not always done my best or even as well as I could have . . . but what I did is done. I must now consign the past to your judgment and accept whatever evaluation the Lord makes of this part of my life when I stand before the Judgment Seat of Christ. I trust God will give me the grace to live the rest of my life so as not to detract from or disgrace this honor He and you have extended to me over all these years.

This will be the last time I will lead you to the Communion Table. So, I have given serious consideration to what the focus of this message should be. While looking to the Lord for His guidance, I was awakened early one morning with the startling awareness that every trip to the Communion Table results in us being justified and set free . . . or judged and condemned.

### How we *leave* the Table of the Lord depends on how we *approach* the Table of the Lord

Jesus wants us to come to His Table prepared to judge ourselves so He can justify us. When we have the courage to do this, then He can set us free from the sins and hurts we have put under His blood and help us leave a Communion service feeling the joy of being forgiven and justifed . . . celebrating the hope of our resurrection and His promised return.

However, the task of judging ourselves is very intimidating. It threatens our peace and makes us fear the loss of others' respect. Like Adam, we would rather hide behind the fig leaves of our own accomplishments and our status. Humbling ourselves before one another does not come easy for us. And there is certainly little peer pressure to encourage us—because everyone else is prone to doing the same thing we would rather do.

If we can forget about what other people will think of us long enough for God's will to prevail in this Communion service, we will leave justified. However, if our stubborn will and the need to protect our pride prevails, we will leave this Communion service under His judgment and condemnation. We may try to shrug off that nagging sense of having unfinished business at the Table of the Lord and pretend that everything is okay between us and our Lord . . . but down inside where no one can see, we know things aren't quite right.

### Rehearsing for heaven at the Table of the Lord

Looked at another way, every trip to the Communion Table gives us an additional opportunity to rehearse for our appearance before the Judgment Seat of Christ when He will judge our works to see whether they can withstand His refining fire. The more honest we are in judging ourselves at the Table of the Lord, the more rewarded and less disappointed we will be at the Judgment Seat of Christ.

Neglecting to judge ourselves at Communion not only results in our chastening here; but also in great disappointment at the Judgment

Seat of Christ. At that time, none of us will be able to avoid or ignore the truth about the life we have lived on earth. God's mercy and grace will spare us the condemnation of the world. Our salvation will be secure. However, the foolish priorities of our life and our unwillingness to face the task of honestly judging ourselves—however unpleasant that task may be—will force us to see our time on earth go up in smoke like so much wood, hay, and stubble. We will live forever with whatever evaluation Christ makes of our life on that day. However, when we regularly and painfully judge ourselves and evaluate our lives at Communion, we escape our Lord's judgment and secure His eternal reward.

How are we to go about judging and evaluating ourselves? What things should we judge? First of all . . .

### We should judge ourselves according to Scripture

Hebrews 4:12,13 reminds us that the Word of God is the only reliable tool for discerning the spiritual origin of the thoughts and intents of the human heart:

> *"For the word of God is quick, and powerful, and sharper than any two-edged sword, piercing even to the dividing asunder of soul and spirit, and of the joints and marrow, and is a discerner of the thoughts and intents of the heart. Neither is there any creature that is not manifest in his sight: but all things are naked and opened unto the eyes of him with whom we have to do."*

Only as we study Scripture and commit it to memory do we have an objective way to determine how obediently or disobediently we are living. David reminds us of this in Psalm 119:9-11:

> *"Wherewithal shall a young man cleanse his way? by taking heed thereto according to thy word. With my whole heart have I sought thee: O let me not wander from thy commandments. Thy word have I hid in mine heart, that I might not sin against thee."*

Later in that same Psalm, in verses 101-106, David observes,

> *"I have refrained my feet from every evil way, that I might keep thy word. I have not departed from thy judgments:*

*for thou hast taught me. How sweet are thy words unto my taste!*
*yea, sweeter than honey to my mouth! Through thy precepts I*
*get understanding: therefore I hate every false way. Thy word is*
*a lamp unto my feet, and a light unto my path. I have sworn, and*
*I will perform it, that I will keep thy righteous judgments."*

When you apply what you know of God's Word to your actions and attitudes as well as to the thoughts and intents of your heart, what conclusions do you reach about how you are living? If we would avoid being judged and chastened by our Lord, we must judge ourselves by the Scriptures.

## We should judge ourselves by
## the saints who have gone before us

What does it mean to be a saint? In the Old Testament, two different Hebrew words are used when referring to saints: *qaddish*, and *chasid*.

*Qaddish* is a word that comes from the Hebrew *qadosh*, which means "holy." To be holy is to dedicate yourself to God and separate yourself from evil. So, saints are "holy." They are people who try to live separate from evil and dedicated to God.

*Chasid*, the other Hebrew word for "saint," means "to be kind or merciful." So, kindness and mercy toward others identify people who are saints.

The New Testament introduces the Greek word *hagios* to describe saints. *Hagios* comes from the Greek word for "holy" and carries a connotation similar to the Hebrew word *qaddish*.

In the New Testament, anyone who believes Jesus Christ is Lord is referred to as a saint. So, a saint is one who bears true and faithful witness to Christ in his or her speech and lifestyle.

Now let's recap. Saints are people who try to live separate from evil and dedicated to God. They are kind and merciful toward others. They bear true and faithful witness to Christ in their speech and lifestyle.

Saints are to serve as spiritual examples or *role models* for us. They are the people whose lives we need to know well enough to copy our attitudes and behaviors from them. That's what role models are, and the reason you will often hear that "modeling" is such a powerful form of teaching is that we generally become like those with whom we spend the most time; those we know best. They are our *role models*. And as we approach the Communion Table this morning, one of the ways I would like for each of us to judge the kind of life we are living is by looking at three groups of saints.

### Old Testament saints

In the eleventh chapter of Hebrews, the writer parades before us several models of faith from the Old Testament. Some are noted for the way they lived. Others' lives are preserved for us because of the way they died. Speaking of those who were stoned, sewn up in animal skins, sawn asunder, and consigned to wander in the deserts and live in dens and caves of the mountains, the Hebrews writer said these were people *"Of whom the world was not worthy."*[5]

These are among the saints who encompass us and are presently witnessing the way we define sainthood in our day. When we judge the way we are reflecting our faith by the way they reflected theirs, how do we measure up?

### New Testament saints

The New Testament is filled with both positive and negative examples of first century Christians. Today, in the presence of the Lord, many of them are celebrating the rewards of our Lord's approval. Others, however, are saddened as they reflect on the regrets of lost opportunities. As we bring ourselves to the judgment of the Lord's Table, which of these groups do our lives most resemble?

In our own modern pilgrimage, we have all observed certain of God's people we look up to and admire and others we view with contempt or with very little respect. What is it that you admire in some of your fellow believers? What are the Christlike qualities they exhibit in their daily walk with Him? What are the qualities you dislike or view unfavorably? How do these measure up against Scripture?

Into which of these groups would you put yourself? If you could ask believers who know you to honestly tell you into which of these groups they would place you, what do you think they would say?

## We should judge ourselves by our Savior

That day in Athens when Paul stood on Mars' Hill confronting the arrogance of Greek wisdom and the ignorance of Greek idolatry, he said,

> *"And the times of this ignorance God winked at; but now commandeth all men everywhere to repent: Because he hath appointed a day, in the which he will judge the world in righteousness by that man whom he hath ordained; whereof he hath given assurance unto all men, in that he hath raised him from the dead."*[6]

The institutional church tends to encourage us to judge ourselves by ourselves and compare ourselves with ourselves. This usually results in self-exaltation or self-justification, rather than in self-judgment.

Paul exposes this problem in addressing the rise of spiritual elitism among some ministers and laity in the Corinthian church. He writes in 2 Corinthians 10:12, *"For we dare not make ourselves of the number, or compare ourselves with some that commend themselves: but they measuring themselves by themselves, and comparing themselves among themselves, are not wise."*

This kind of comparison breeds the pride and competition that create so much suspicion and mistrust among us. Such a false sense of measurement or judgment tends to cause some of us to think of ourselves as winners and others as losers in the ministry.

## The true measure of a steward's achievement

Faithfulness, not success, is the standard by which we should measure our service for the Lord. The success standard by which the institutional church extends its recognition—success—is a faulty and unreliable measure. Positions and plaques are enjoyable, but they will mean little or nothing at the Judgment Seat of Christ. God doesn't see us like others see us. He doesn't judge us as others do. People look on the outside of us, but God looks straight into our heart.

The Communion Table is the most important cardiac center in the world. And the world's greatest cardiologist is here. He knows whose heart needs medication. He knows whose heart needs surgery. However, if He is going to help us, we must put ourselves in His hands. Today, He is the Great Physician. At the Judgment Seat of Christ, He will be the Awesome Judge. The more often we approach Him for medication and/ or surgery, the less painful we will find our trip to the Judgment Seat of Christ.

Paul reminds us in Acts 17:31, just as he did the Athenians on Mars' Hill, that there is coming, *"A day, in the which he will judge the world in righteousness by that man whom he hath ordained."* In one way or another, Jesus Christ will judge every human being.

### The judgment of the unbeliever

The unbeliever will be judged by whether or not he is *in* Christ. Those who have not accepted Christ's sacrifice as atonement for their sin are not in Christ. So, at the Great White Throne Judgment, they will have to stand judgment for their sins. Thank God, Christ has delivered us from that day!

### The judgment of the believer

Believers will be judged by the degree to which we are *like* Christ. This will occur, as Paul reminds us, at the Judgment Seat of Christ: *". . . we must all appear before the judgment seat of Christ; that every one may receive the things done in his body, according to that he hath done, whether it be good or bad"* (2 Corinthians 5:10).

He further admonishes us, in Romans 14:10-13,

> *"But why dost thou judge thy brother? or why dost thou set at nought thy brother? for we shall all stand before the judgment seat of Christ. For it is written, As I live, saith the Lord, every knee shall bow to me, and every tongue shall confess to God. So then every one of us shall give account of himself to God. Let us not therefore judge one another any more . . . ."*

In 1 Corinthians 3:12-15, Paul also says,

> *"Now if any man build upon this foundation gold, silver, precious stones, wood, hay, stubble; Every man's work shall be made manifest: for the day shall declare it, because it shall be revealed by fire; and the fire shall try every man's work of what*

*sort it is. If any man's work abide which he hath built thereupon, he shall receive a reward. If any man's work shall be burned, he shall suffer loss: but he himself shall be saved; yet so as by fire."*

On that day, God will judge us by the degree to which we have used the opportunities He has given to us to grow into *"the measure of the stature of the fulness of Christ"* (Ephesians 4:13). In other words, we will be measured by how much we have become like Christ.

## Judgment occurs with every trip to the Table of the Lord

May God make each of us aware that every time we come to the Communion Table and partake of the emblems of our Lord's broken body and His shed blood, judgment occurs. If we do not judge ourselves, the Lord will judge us. If we refuse to respond to the guilt and condemnation he incites within us, then we will continue to harden our hearts. We will suffer deeper depression, greater loss of self-respect, and there will be no relief in the complications of our lives and relationships.

Jesus wants us to judge ourselves. Whenever we judge ourselves . . . confess our sins . . . repent of them . . . realize He was judged for them so that we can leave His table justified and free to live without guilt, knowing that because God sees us through the blood of Christ, we appear before His Presence *as though we had never sinned.*

While the brethren come to serve us Communion, I want us to sing some hymns that will encourage us to bring ourselves to judgment so we can leave with our Lord's justification. First, let's sing "There's Room at the Cross for You." And let's sing it for each other as though each of us is saying to the other, "I'm going to Calvary with my sins today, and there's room for you there, too."

Then, I'd like to hear us sing, "Just As I Am." This is often used as an invitation to unbelievers, but it speaks directly to the heart of every believer. And, if you know the story of this hymn and Charlotte Elliott, its author, it is obvious that it was written by someone who had made many trips to the Table of the Lord and examined herself carefully in the Lord's presence. An invalid for the last 62 of her 82 years on earth, she was determined to live a life that would show others that, "God sees, God guides, and God guards me. His grace surrounds me, and His voice continually bids me to be happy and holy in His service just where I am." [7] She wrote the text to help her brother, a pastor, cover the expenses of a school he was building for the children of poor clergymen in their hometown of Brighton, England.

Records indicate that this hymn from the pen of the pastor's invalid sister brought in more funds than all of his combined efforts at fund-raising. When she died, family and friends found over a thousand letters from people all over the world expressing what this hymn had meant in their lives. And she was able to write those words that rang so true to others' hearts because she had spiritually, if not physically, been to the "Table of the Lord" over and over in her own life, examining herself and measuring herself against her Lord and Savior Jesus Christ.

Now, let's sing, "When I Survey the Wondrous Cross." And we'll conclude with, "On Christ, the Solid Rock I Stand."

---

[1] Romans 2:1-16.
[2] Psalm 44:20,21.
[3] 1 Corinthians 11:26-32.
[4] Romans 5:1.
[5] Hebrews 11:38.
[6] Acts 17:30.
[7] Osbeck, Kenneth W. **101 Hymn Stories.** Grand Rapids, Michigan: Kregel Publications, 1982, p. 146-7.